Cheap Chic

CHIC

UPDATE

by
Caterine Milinaire
and Carol Troy

Revised edition by Carol Troy

Designed by Bea Feitler

Harmony Books
New York

Design Assistant: Carl Barile
Research: Martha Siegler, Diane Partie
Cover Lettering: Barbara Richer
Cover Photograph of Yasmine courtesy Pinky and Dianne Ltd.

Harmony Books, a division of Crown Publishers, Inc.
One Park Avenue, New York, New York 10016
Published simultaneously in Canada by General Publishing Company Limited.
Printed in the United States of America.

Library of Congress Cataloging in Publication Data

Milinaire, Caterine.
Cheap chic update

1. Fashion.   2. Clothing and dress.
I. Troy, Carol, joint author.   II. Title.
TT515.M59 1978   646'.34   78-4148
ISBN 0-517-53460-6
ISBN 0-517-53456-8 pbk.

TABLE OF CONTENTS

dedicated to

maurice   hogenboom

from caterine

RAGS

Mary Peacok

Carol Troy

For Mary and every body who's worked so long and hard on Rags magazine!

And with love to Lucian K. Truscott IV —Carol Troy 1978

INTRODUCTION

You might be interested in the story of this little pink book and how it came to pass. Since it was written for you, you have a right to know.

Three years ago, when *Cheap Chic* was first published, I really took it on the chin from Barbara Walters. The "Today" Show was the first time I'd ever been on television, and I was scared to death. She stuck it to me, and I guess I didn't hold up my end too well. *Cheap Chic*, she said, was written only for skinny young girls who didn't have jobs.

Well, it looks like Barbara Walters was wrong. Because three years later we're coming out with a new *Cheap Chic*. The pictures have changed here and there, but the words remain pretty much the same. Because despite Barbara Walters, this book had some basic truths in it. Some truths about finding out who you are and being faithful to that person. Finding out what *you* like and feel good wearing, and hanging on to it. To me, this is the *real* way to dress for success. To feel it from the inside. Because what is style all about but wearing your insides on your outsides? And if we can tell you in *Cheap Chic* some of the sly ways of looking chic on the cheap, all the better. The real bottom line here is not dollars and cents: it's how you feel about yourself. Sure, we know you can't wear jeans to the office. If you're a career woman, you're going to be more interested in the Classics chapter than the Wrapping chapter...but maybe you'll love tying on a pareo when you take a well-deserved vacation! So there's something 9 for everybody—and everybody, young or old, rich or poor, tall or short, slender or hefty—can find something good and useful in this book.

You don't have to lock up your wallet when you go shopping *Cheap Chic* style. The stuff in this book applies to a trip to Bloomingdale's, Neiman-Marcus, or I. Magnin, as well as to a trip to Woolworth's. We're merely encouraging you to embrace your own style and express your own individuality with confidence. You have the freedom to sidestep designer dictatorship and make the clothes you spend your money on work for *you*, rather than making *you* work for your clothes.

—Carol Troy/1978

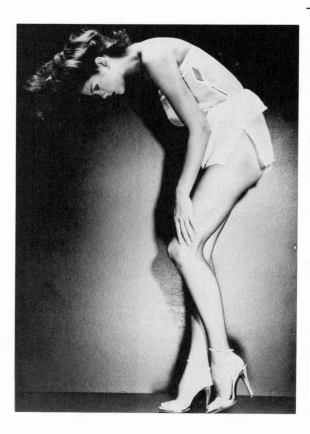

The most basic element of Cheap Chic is the body you hang your clothes on. Building a healthy, lively body is far cheaper than buying a lot of clothes to distract from it. And once you really know your flesh and bones, you'll find it easier to choose the clothes you really need and love.

Try standing in front of a full-length mirror some morning, not holding in your stomach, tightening your buttocks, or sticking out your chest. Take a look at your body—front, side, and back. Are you content with what you see? Is your skin clear and healthy? Could the muscle tone of your stomach, upper arms, and thighs be firmed up with a little jogging, swimming, or a ten-block walk each morning? It isn't important if your breasts, hips, or legs aren't those you would see in a fashion magazine or in the pages of *Playboy*. What matters is that you get acquainted with them as they are and treat them with care and respect.

There are no secret recipes for keeping your body together, but learning to take a certain pleasure in self-discipline is a first step... discipline in eating and sleeping habits that helps build good emotional and physical relationships. Once you decide to perk up your body, there are many ways to go about it: Invent your own exercises and treatments, seek advice from a friend who enjoys and studies physical movement, find a class you like, read body books, and keep trying different ways until you find a routine that really feels comfortable for you...one you can really stick with. Diana Vreeland, after almost forty years with *Harper's Bazaar* and *Vogue*, describes the secrets of a vibrant woman: "You have to have a sense of pleasure and a sense of discipline to look really well. You have to have a sound, athletic body, lead a busy life, and worry less. Live correctly and take risks."

Once you have a body program set up, start having fun with your clothes. Perhaps the best place to start thinking about the evocative nature of fabric, color, and clothes is with the senses:

Touch: the softness of washed cottons, thick velvets, tender cashmeres, bumpy corduroys; the harshness of raw wool.

Smell: the scent of a real leather bag versus imitation leather; a wet wool sweater versus a polyester knit.

Sound: the rustle of taffeta, the squawk of rubbers in the rain, the flapping of canvas, the whisper of nylons.

Sight: the harmonious blends of bright or subtle colors, rough and smooth textures, straight and curved silhouettes.

Now, with all your senses in full gear, let's take a look into the world of Cheap Chic.

FIRST LAYERS

There's one very good reason for stocking up on the basics: peace of mind. You'll *never* have to get up in the early morning darkness and stumble about looking for something to match up with something else. If you've got the basics, they're all interchangeable—T-shirts, turtlenecks, or cotton shirts; and with them several pair of jeans, green GI pants, white pants, and a wide skirt. It's rather like wearing a second skin, but more colorful! The reassuring thing about having a drawerful of these things is that you can stick any top with any bottom and it will look great. How can you miss with solid colors, basic quality, simple cut

and time-tested designs? And what feels better than slipping into a freshly laundered cotton outfit in your favorite color, tying on a scarf, and giving it no more thought? If you hate to think about what you're putting on your back, and refuse to spend any time messing about with your "wardrobe," you're all set with the basics. You'll have all the more time to get down to what you really want to achieve in life rather than spending hours shopping in department stores and dressing up in a "fashion statement" or a "look for fall." In the basics, you can remain anonymous, observe and stalk the life you're after in a quiet and individual style.

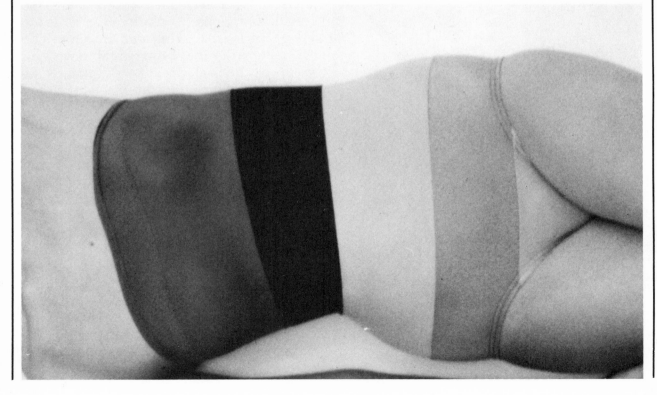

JEANS AND OTHER COVERINGS

One good friend of ours who dresses like a modern-day John Wayne professes to care nothing, or very little, about the clothes he wears. And yet he combs the city to find the precise pair of **jeans** he wants—Lees. Why? Because jeans, like almost everything else, have fallen prey to the fashion cycle. You can find bell-bottomed jeans, boot-leg jeans, even flared jeans. But just try to find a regular, trusty old pair of straight-legged denim jeans with no frills. Our friend has looked in Columbus, Ohio (Surely the farmers would have them!), in Chicago, Illinois, and in Binghamton, New York. His only dependable source: Kauffman's Riding Store in New York City. Jeans are such a totem of American culture that they inspire that kind of mania for the marginal differences, for the tiny details that will set you off from the crowd, set you apart from the blue-legged masses.

First layers: everything from leotards to Levi's can keep you going from morning 'til night with a minimal investment of time and money.

Forty-Niners at the Last Chance Mine, 1882, wearing riveted Levi's and sturdy boots that look like today's Frye boots.

In the fifties, jeans were good as gold behind the Iron Curtain: to the Russians they summed up all the romantic promise of the American frontier, the wildness of the West. Like nylons in World War II, jeans were great for bartering and bribing. The Levi trademark—that little red tab sewn into the side of the back pocket—is registered in sixty countries including Russia, where they don't even make jeans.

Originally, jeans were coveted in Paris, and then Yves St. Laurent came along and knocked them off in couture. The French have taken the basic idea of blue jeans, restyled and recut them for that tight European fit . . . and now they sell like crazy in America at twice the original price. It's typical of the French to pick up basic American design and transform it with colorings and proportion into something quintessentially Parisian, something almost like a national uniform.

A good basic pair of jeans will last several years, mold themselves to your body, and fade with style. Like all good clothes,

Cher, wearing a pair of jeans that fit the way jeans should fit.

they improve with age. In the summer, you can cut them off into shorts; in the winter, open the seams of the legs, set in a piece of denim, and have a warm, long skirt.

The price of jeans is going up, due to world-wide demand for denim, but they remain one of the central American classics.

Once you find a brand of jeans that fits you the way you like to be fit, stick with it. Plan on the waist and inseam shrinking about 8 percent. Levi-Strauss boot-leg jeans are cut shorter in the front of the leg and longer in the back so they'll look good over Frye boots, cowboy boots, or any boots with

Sasson, like Fiorucci, Jesus Jeans, etc., is just one of the many European jeans cut tight, tight!

heels. Straight-legged Lees have an easy fit and fly front, whereas Wranglers come in a more malleable denim that takes less breaking-in but is less durable. You can choose a less sturdy, less expensive brand like Wayfarers or Landlubbers, which don't last a lifetime but are easily settled into. Once you've settled on your best size and brand, it's sometimes easier to buy them already worn at a swap meet rather than breaking them in yourself. Or, as John Burks noted in a book about jeans, "When you're rich you have them pre-bleached and pressed. Bleached Levi's: upward mobility."

Jeans come in all styles and colors these days, but beware! Stick with straight legs or pegged legs without cuffs, and avoid jeans cut very low on the hips. Even jeans can do you in with supermarket overchoice. Stick to the basics because that "fashion detailing," like industrial-zipper-fly fronts, is going to tire real fast.

If you've never been fond of jeans, consider buying a few pair of green **Army fatigue pants** with the pockets on the sides. All over Europe, fashionable girls are wearing them tucked into the tops of their high leather boots or with a pair of patterned socks and loafers. The fabric is the best, and the U.S. Army is easily the equal of the

Levi-Strauss Company when it comes to putting together a totally functional, beautifully designed piece of clothing.

If you don't relish the thought of marching around looking like a Vietnam vet in jungle green pants, there's yet another alternative—white pants. You can buy white jeans, English or American sailor pants, or painter's pants.

Sailor pants have wide, straight legs and come in a tightly woven long-lasting cotton twill with buttoned closings. They should run about $6 if they're truly "surplus" and not some slyly manufactured imitation. And if they are the real thing, you'll find they take dye beautifully because of their pure cotton fiber.

The first time we saw white **painter's pants** was in a "street fashion" photograph in the Los Angeles *Times*. You can find them at Standard Brands Paints in Los Angeles for 69¢, or in boutiques for several times that. They're a great buy, with all

Twenty years ago
James Dean
seemed stylishly alienated in well-worn denim jeans and a tattered cotton shirt. Today, jeans still have a whiff of the rebel about them . . . not without cause.

realize how really nice they feel on the legs and how charming they look to others. A tight skirt isn't really practical in this era of constant movement, but is fun to wear in the evening with a big T-shirt or man's shirt

Designer Ola Hudson puts scissors, pins, markers and measuring tapes in the pockets of her sturdy white painter's pants and rotates different long-sleeved cotton T-shirts. With a drawer full of pants and T-shirts, she never has to worry about what to wear to work in the morning.

sorts of mysterious pockets, straps, and tabs designed for the house-painter's craft. A designer in North Hollywood, who could choose to wear any of her luxurious designs, seems to wear nothing but painter's pants and T-shirts under her forties-look velour jackets and coats.

Of course, now that everyone's been wearing pants as a daily routine, there's a strong feeling in the air for **skirts.** We're over the boring, burning issue of how long a skirt should be, and can lean back and

Peter Hujar's uniform: jeans, an army-surplus leather belt, and a crocodile shirt (without the crocodile).

18

Lauren Hutton's favorite style: jeans, a roomy man's shirt and a pastel Shetland sweater. 19

on top and high strappy shoes on your feet. And if pants make you feel uncomfortable, get several skirts. You can find gathered, circle, pleated, or soft A-lines, reasonably priced, at department stores and boutiques. Get two or three in the right colors and you're all set. (A warning: beware of linen if you don't like irons.)

COTTON T-SHIRTS AND OTHER WONDERS

The cheapest mate for your jeans and skirts is a plain cotton T-shirt, so be sure to keep a good supply. A T-shirt in solid colors and different styles can take you through all the seasons. Once you've got a few in your drawer, you'll see how useful and dependable they are.

When you do find your favorite T-shirt, be sure to buy several. Cheap chic doesn't necessarily mean really cheap—spend your money when you find the best style for you.

Buy in multiples, because this is one situation where less is not more. With five perfect T-shirts and three pair of perfectly fitting pants or skirts, you ought to stay happily clothed for quite a while.

There is the **cheap, short-sleeved T-shirt** or the undershirt-style T-shirt that comes in white and pastels from discount and dime stores. Often you can find three packaged for $4.98. If they are dyed they look terrific (a dusty rose, for instance, tucked into tight olive pants and high boots). The pastels, like pale sky blue and sunny yellow, are fresh clean colors for summer: they look fine as a skinny-minny T-shirt at the beach. There's nothing like a fresh pastel cotton T-shirt and a warm, mellow touch of sun to make you feel great.

One way to wear these freshly dyed $2 T-shirts is like New York's Puerto Rican kids do in Central Park in the summer: the girls buy extralarge sizes, grab a handful of fabric on either side of the chest, pull it supertight, and make a knot in the front, along the lines of a calypso shirt bodice. It

20   **A T-shirt, with a touch of lace at the neck, dresses up a softly gathered skirt.**

To dye your T-shirt, try Andrea Quinn's recipes with Rit dyes for smokier, sun-bleached colors:

• Burnt Orange: ¼ teaspoon each of Golden Yellow, Orange, Chestnut Brown, and Dark Brown.
• Plum: 1 teaspoon Wine, ¼ teaspoon Charcoal Grey, and ¼ teaspoon Cocoa Brown.
• Fuzzy Green: ½ teaspoon Dark Green and ½ teaspoon Charcoal Grey.
• Blue Smoke: generous ½ teaspoon Navy Blue and skimpy ½ teaspoon Charcoal Grey.
• Mocha Chocolate: generous ½ teaspoon Pink and skimpy ½ teaspoon Dark Brown.

To dye a clean white cotton T-shirt, put on a pair of rubber gloves, line a hand strainer with a paper towel, and put in the dye mix. Hold it under the faucet while you fill the sink with your hottest water, and mix up the water to help it all dissolve. (Undissolved bits of

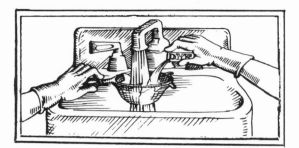

dye will spot your T-shirt.) Then put in a completely wet, clean T-shirt until it turns several shades darker than you want it. It will dry to the color you like (hopefully). The tiny undershirt bows take color faster so dye them separately.

If it comes out a color you don't like, buy some dye remover or stick it back in the basin for a darker color. You can also play with the mix of colors in the shade. To experiment with any colors, mix drops of dissolved dye in a bowl and test the shade with a white paper towel. To dye a skirt or white sailor pants to a matching shade, experiment to find the dye intensity that takes best on that particular fabric.

After you've finished dyeing, dip the clothing into half a cup of vinegar in a sinkful of cold water so the color won't fade. Always wash home-done dye jobs in cold water with a mild soap.

makes for a very narrow, high, tight bust. Cheap Chic! A man's large T-shirt also makes a soft dress to wear at a summer place over a bikini; they even come in handy as swimsuits when you've forgotten yours. Worn over a pair of brightly printed under-

Paul Newman didn't have to dye his undershirt to look like a real peach.

pants or Woolworth's brown $1 "string" bikini, a wet T-shirt can be terribly revealing while protecting you from the sun.

Sometimes you just can't get away with Woolworth's T-shirts, no matter how beautifully they are colored and camouflaged. And it's often very difficult to find plain T-shirts, either long- or short-sleeved. You can buy them with daisies on the front or a laughing cow, or in chartreuse and fuchsia stripes; but start looking for a plain, solid color, well-made cotton version. We once spent three hours doing just that in Chicago. And though it may be discouraging, the only plain T-shirt we came up with was a $12 French model at Jax.

Luckily, many manufacturers have realized recently that women like the idea of T-shirt dressing, and they are turning out new-looking T-shirts that can go to the office tucked into a skirt, then straight òut to a dinner or date after work. These T-shirts are not as tight and often have a gathered or slit neck that can be worn untied after office hours. Loosen the neck, dress up your look with a favorite neck jewel or Woolworth's bangles, and a big hair comb. Blouse the T-shirt over your skirt (or slacks) with a narrow metallic belt, slip on high evening sandals, and you're off. (Just make sure your bag is large enough to carry all your presto-chango gear!)

Ingrid Boulting skips rope in Central Park and then bikes to lunch in her plain black T-shirt and pants.

One of the greatest bargains around is a plain old Fruit of the Loom man's T-shirt. In Europe, they're being worn with the label out. Here, they make the cheapest solution for that big top you're looking for to match up with a loose skirt or tight pants. Try dying them plum, fuzzy green, or blue smoke (see page 21) and wear them over layered, dyed petticoats from a dime store or ordered from a big catalogue.

When it gets chilly, **turtlenecks** are warmer than the basic T-shirt design. Army-surplus stores carry cheap long-sleeved turtlenecks in cotton knits, but they tend to bag, and sometimes the elastic in the cuffs and neck starts to give and curls out of the cotton knit like little worms after a morning rain.

A really sturdy turtleneck is more expensive, perhaps $15, and comes in a stretchy synthetic mix like nylon and Lycra. These fit beautifully, and the neck never gets worn out from all that on-and-off stretching. They're worth the price, but be sure to get

bound seams for your money. When they reach the end of their life, synthetics start to run at the seams, but this isn't for several years of almost daily wearing. A black T-shirt or turtleneck with a pair of black pants can take you almost anyplace, from jogging in the park to dinner at the finest restaurants.

When you're traveling, be sure to pick up a few **tourist T-shirts** for the folks back home. You can find the flashiest styles in the large discount stores of Florida, California, New York, and points between. They have a certain naive exuberance, with their Day-Glo oranges, state maps, and Hollywood fantasies, and they're always made up in cotton. Friends can wear them under or over other T-shirts, or throw out their old pajamas and sleep in a "Florida Sunshine State." A collection of twenty is more than enough to take a person through three changes a day for a week before hitting the washing machine.

For **dress-up T-shirts,** you can transform a scoop neck into a décolleté by gathering the front into a barette-shaped pin between the breasts. Or if you want to really get "steppy" (that's midwestern for fit to kill), buy some cheap, tattered twenties chemises or nightgowns at a thrift shop. You're looking for the lace edgings or beautifully worked pockets. Cut them loose from their old moorings and reapply them to your new T-shirt. With a pair of dusty blue sailor pants dyed to match the top, you've got a fairly delicate evening effect. Or you can stitch on an old piece of fabric or sew a few scarves around the hem of your T-shirt to create a loose and floaty dress.

We're not going to suggest you equip yourself with an embroidery outfit and start some five-hour home project with jeans and T-shirts. We're not getting into crafts, because the idea of Cheap Chic is to save on both the money and the time you invest. We figure that anyone who's sharp enough to buy this book isn't sitting around spending huge amounts of their time "saving money" with homey handiworks when they could be out making the money to save them the time. (Make the money, buy yourself time. *Then* you can dawdle with crafts to your heart's content!)

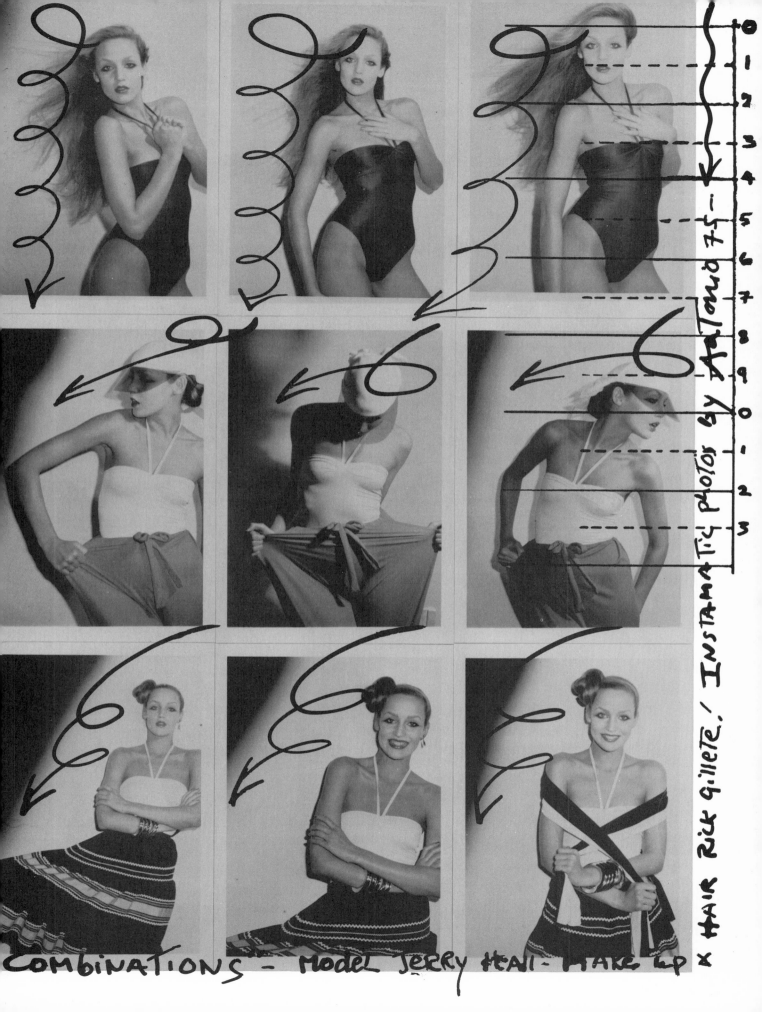

COMBINATIONS - MODEL JERRY HALL - MAKE UP

HAIR RICK GILLETE. / INSTAMATIC PHOTOS BY AYTAND 75-K

LEOTARDS
AND OTHER STRETCHY THINGS

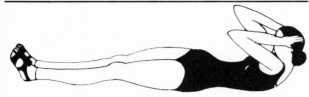

Leotards come in a close second to T-shirts for all-around wearability. They are lightweight, durable, crushproof, quick drying, and they really shape themselves to your body, giving a custom fit at noncustom prices.

A leotard can go under all your basic pants, shirts, and skirts. You can perk it up with a cheap cotton scarf. You can wear it by itself for dancing, exercise, and swimming. And you can pick one up just about anywhere—hosiery shops, dime stores, department stores. Sometimes you can even find a leotard on a rack next to the fruit stand in the supermarket.

A tiny nylon leotard can fit in your pocket for the first ray of sunshine and then take you off to a patch of grass or the seashore. In the summertime, leotards litter the streets of Manhattan. Both Capezio and

Liza Minnelli's outgrown her first Capezios but she still loves to wear leotards . . . even if they are by Halston!

Danskin Classics: the leotards that stepped out to the beach, the disco, the office . . . in shimmery, mouth-watering colors.

Danskin have been at their business a long time and are extremely knowledgeable in the ways of manufacturing a long-lasting, durable product. The locked seams hold together under the stretchiest of stretches. And they come in a great variety of shapes and colors. A recent classic is the Danskin wraparound skirt dyed to match their leotards, perfect for business travel and trips to and from an exercise class. (One small warning: Keep an eye on your layering when you wear a leotard without a snap crotch. The snapless leotards are smoother and healthier, but it takes forever to unpeel yourself in the bathroom!)

If you don't feel comfortable in skintight turtlenecks and T-shirts and leotards, gather up a collection of **loose cotton shirts.** A man's old shirt can look terrific tucked in at the waist over a turtleneck; or, if it's large and straight at the bottom, pulled tight with a wide belt at the waist. If the collar has seen better days, cut it off above the seam where it joins the shirt, turn it under, and sew into place. If the shirttails are too curved, cut them straight and then hem them. A lot of women sneak into the boy's department of Brooks Brothers, the crusty old men's outfitters in New York. When the owners found they were buying boy's shirts to wear, they made one conces-

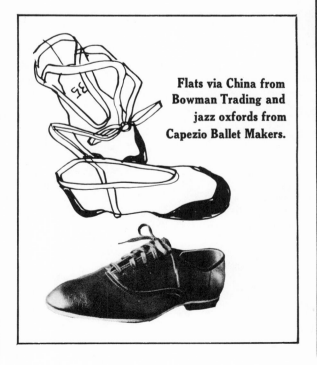

Flats via China from Bowman Trading and jazz oxfords from Capezio Ballet Makers.

Capezio Ballet Makers' one-piece knit camisole jumpsuit—under skirts, loose shirts, long tunics, wide hip-belts, legwarmers—however it feels good on you.

Wendy Whitelaw—New York makeup artist—considers her face the real first layer of her style.

sion: they made up a cotton broadcloth button-down shirt sized for women. But for some reason, the boy's shirts are as popular as ever, perhaps because of that loose, low-arm-holed look and those pure cottons you'd pay four times as much for in other stores (if you could find them). And you can order them easily by mail.

So choose your skirts, pants, and tops very carefully. Now, sit back and relax. You can stop reading this book right here, and if you happen to live in a warm climate, you'll have enough clothes to take you through the whole year.

THE LAYER ESCALATION

One woman who has made a total discipline out of dressing around the basics is Helene Gaillet, a New York photojournalist. Her working day usually starts at eight sharp and keeps her running until six or often seven at night. Since she has little time to change from working clothes to evening clothes, she's eliminated dress-up clothes as much as possible from her wardrobe. She works at such an intense pitch that she has to be very careful about keeping both her body and her clothes in perfect running order. Her clothes are now so few and so honed down that when she travels, she takes only one duffel bag, which fits under the airplane seat in front of her. Here are her rules.

This gold and leather English cavalry belt has been worn with jeans every other day for over ten years and it looks better now than ever.

The monogrammed boy's shirt is a basic element in Helene Gaillet's special system of year-round layering.

"Ninety-five percent of my clothes are in navy blue, white, or khaki. I never go shopping, and when I do, I know specifically what I want. I have an $80 or $100 bill a year plus shoes, and that's it.

"I buy my jeans in shades of blue at the army-navy store. They're always Levi's, often in corduroy. The Levi cut is thinner—they seem to cut Wranglers for big asses and Levi's for almost nonexistent asses! Levi's are cut straight and never need to be tailored to fit me.

"I wear the same shirt all year round, even when I'm skiing. It's the layer theory: one, two, three, or four things go on top of each other. My cotton turtlenecks go under the shirt—they're $6 at the army-navy store, or $15 in an imported stretch acrylic fabric. I get the little-boy's button-down oxford shirt from Brooks Brothers in three colors—white, the blue stripe, and yellow—a dozen at a time every three years. They're $11 plus $5 for the initials, and that way it looks

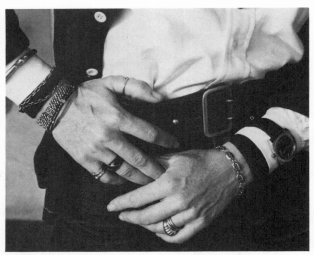

An inexpensive shirt, jeans, a belt and overshirt are complemented by Helene's collection of gold jewelry.

like you're wearing a $60 custom shirt. Then I have three good silk shirts, all in ivory white. My oldest one is eight years . . . I got it on sale for $50. But they usually only last two or three years, because they get yellowish with dry cleaning.

"Boots are one of my most expensive items because I literally live in them. I get one or two pair a year and wear them over three or four years. They're usually English or French. My pant boots are $90 from Veneziano, but I usually buy St. Laurent boots; one pair long, the other short to go under jeans, and they run around $150 a pair. I've found the trick to keeping jeans tucked into your boots—fit a pair of bright red 69¢ socks from Woolworth's over your pant legs with tights underneath. I love wearing bright red underthings!

"To go with the tops and jeans, I have just three belts that I bought in the sixties: an old leather army belt from the flea market in Paris, a Turkish metal belt from an antique store, and a gold-and-leather English cavalry belt from the Chelsea Antique Market that I wear about every other day. They were all under $20.

"My everyday winter outfit is my jeans, turtleneck, shirt, and T-shirt, plus a fisherman's sweater from the Fulton Street Fish Market, a belt, and usually a long, thrift-shop scarf. If it's really cold, I add a $6 safari jacket from the army-navy store. And

The ins-and-outs of the over-and-under school of dressing: Helene puts on a T-shirt, a boy's shirt, a denim overshirt, tucks it all into jeans and a pair of good leather boots and then relaxes.

always boots, a canvas camera bag (actually a game bag, which was a gift, because I think they're too expensive), a $2 denim hat from the dime store, and a pair of sunglasses.

"In the summer I wear cutoffs, Cloroxed $11 Wayfarer jeans, and T-shirts I can throw in the washing machine. If it gets cold, I put on a denim shirt.

"I just don't buy expensive things, except boots."

"For evening wear, I've worked out a 'tuxedo'—eight-year-old wool gabardine St. Laurent pants copied by Alexander's department store with a black velvet jacket from a boutique, plus a vest and cheap satin shirt. I wear it with strapped sandals and flaming red tights, and the red toes peek out from under all the black!

"I do sink money in accessories: I always wear the same ones, and I do spend on them. I've got a five-year-old brown suede pouch from La Bagagerie. All my gold things have been stolen twice, so I don't have much left: five rings, a Cartier tank watch with a clasp that cost $600 in Paris eight years ago, a Van Cleef and Arpels bracelet, and some gold chains. They're like good-luck charms. I even swim and sleep with them on.

"In the last year I've gone from 124 pounds to around 118 at five foot six. My secret is a small breakfast: a glass of orange juice, four cups of very strong espresso, and a toasted English muffin. I eat lunch less than once a week, and when I do, try to make it Japanese. And then I eat anything for dinner, but very little. That way I never diet!

"I go to an exercise class twice a week. I spend my money there and on having my hair streaked. And I've done the Royal Canadian Air Force exercises ten minutes every morning since 1962. I save money on cabs by doing everything on my bike or on foot; and year round I play tennis and ski. I'd love to be one of the great beauties, but, to make the best of myself, I have to radiate what I can get from inside: health. I think your mental attitude is based on your physical well-being."

Ballet clothes become fashion shows: Rudi Gernreich's "tunic" panelled leotard for disco dancing.

GILDA RADNER

Saturday Night Lively!

Gilda Radner, one of the Glamour Queens of "Saturday Night Live," talks about her off-camera fashion style. What does she base her particular taste in clothes on? "What doesn't itch."

"I think I've always been ahead of fashion. I tucked my pants into my boots years ago, mainly because they were usually too short. And I've always worn clothes in layers 'cause it seemed there was always something to hide. Now, in fashion, I think I prefer the classic, peasant, layered look: clothes that don't match that you could wear to any country on top of each other.

"In the morning I choose my clothes by what's clean . . . also, I think clothes should feel safe. I just like clothes you could want to go to sleep in. I sometimes stand in front of the mirror and change a million times because I know I really want to wear my nightgown. So I guess I associate clothes with home and comfort. I don't have a wardrobe. I have a history. Things that went through stuff with me.

"The clothes I hate are the ones that let me down. You know, the ones that are never the same after the first washing. I hate materials that retain perspiration that you know you didn't make yourself. The ones you always have to smell before you wear or pour a lot of perfume on. And I hated thigh chafe guards as a kid . . . I've weighed up to 150 pounds and I'm five feet six. I lost weight by being on every diet I've ever heard of or read about or had passed to me on a mimeographed piece of paper. I'm a compulsive eater, and the only way to stay thin when you're a compulsive eater is to be just as compulsive about losing weight.

"TV hasn't changed my life too much, but it's changed my hair. I used to wear it in a style . . . all curly around my face. I used to hide somewhere in there, but then they told me they couldn't see my face at all when I turned to the side on TV. So I started pulling it off my face. Then I stopped setting it and started rolling it into a little knot. That was the first time I actually got a good look at my face and decided it was a regular face, not beautiful, but at least I looked like a real person on TV. With all this new self-acceptance, it takes a lot less time to get ready in the morning.

"My favorite accessory? My contacts. Because if I didn't wear them I'd have to wear big, thick glasses. And I like shoes that make your feet look cute, like puppy paws. And high heels if they make your legs look long. A guy once told me I had long legs; so I capitalized on them by wearing high heels. Unfortunately, I also have a small head . . . the longer I make my legs, the smaller my head looks .

"Exercise? In the morning I do a hundred jumping jacks, then I do a hundred skip ropes. Then I make the bed, picking up the pillows off the floor without bending my knees. There are four pillows. Then I do thirty leg lifts and thirty bum walks, backward and forward. Then I take a bath and think about whether I should add another exercise to my regime."

CLASSICS

Sometimes Cheap Chic boils down to spending much more than you feel you can afford on the kind of classic, quality clothes we talk about in this chapter. We think it saves you money in the long run. If you're a real purist, Cheap Chic can become a matter of extremes: throwing your last $150 into a tweed riding jacket and riding out poverty in style. But if you don't feel comfortable investing in truly expensive classics, then consider buying some of the second-string classics we'll be talking about in the next chapter, like a lovely Shetland sweater or cowboy boots.

There are still certain things you shouldn't fudge on no matter how cheaply you dress: the very best boots, a sturdy bag, a glorious jacket or shirt. You can't afford cheap boots that will last a year and then crack across the sole. If you had loads of money you could; but since you don't, spend your money where it shows the most.

If you look closely at a woman with a strong individual style, you will discover there is almost always something in her outfit that costs a lot. Perhaps it's a five-year-old pair of French boots or a simple, solid-gold chain around her wrist. Whatever it is, that one touch makes her look ten times better. The throwaway chic gives her an intriguing look.

It might seem impossible to think of yourself laying out $150 on a pair of boots. If so, start saving, even if it's only $5 a week. If you can't manage that, then stop smoking, and start eating soybean protein! In five years you'll still be wearing those boots (inflation will then have jacked them up to $300) and they will look beautifully, aristocratically worn and weathered. They'll save

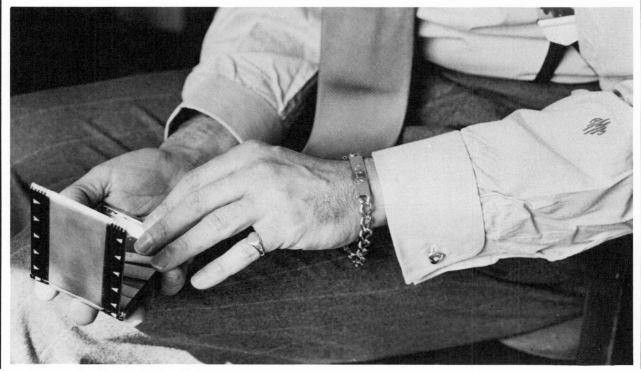

A well tailored suit can last decades. Antonio Lopez's suit is made of black cashmere by Cifonelli in Paris.

your wardrobe with a cheeky touch of class even when you're really hard up and down to your last pair of jeans.

This is a very European way of dressing. French designer Emmanuelle Khanh thinks that the great thing about France is the *bon gout*, the good taste. "It's a process of refining that's been going on for centuries. We're more moderate and appreciate quality, so our clothes last longer. Since we don't exaggerate our appearance, we have more balance in choosing our personal styles. At first it may look as if we're wearing a uniform, but then you notice the subtle differences in shades, cuts, and quality of fabric. An older woman is often seen in what a girl of eighteen buys because it's all based on classic proportion."

You can keep a very small closet if you're careful, almost ruthless, in choosing your few classic investments. Tina Bossidy, a nine-to-five fashion editor in New York, has it down to a system. She believes in that old fashion-magazine idea of "setting up a wardrobe." It sounds terribly stuffy, because we haven't needed the discipline to think this way for a long time. But the results can be great—a group of clothes that are not faddy, that are not going to pass out of style, and that you can build up year after year. What this plan involves, again, is a much smaller, more thought-out wardrobe. Here are some of her tips.

• **Color** is the most important thing in dressing well. The whole point of looking good is feeling good, so find the colors that make you feel best and stick with them. Women often forget they look very good in soft colors, like a light turquoise. Try it.
• One of the big mistakes is buying **prints.** If you develop your sense of color and buy mainly solids, everything will work together.
• A big secret is to buy things in **multiples.** Once you find your favorite colors, the easiest thing to do is to set up a sort of *uniform* of top quality: For instance, buy six mens' silk shirts when they go on sale: blue, red, black, green, maroon, turquoise, and purple. Buy two identical skirts: purple and black. Department stores usually overbuy. If something falls into the uniform category, then it will probably go on sale in three weeks to a month, even at the designer boutiques. Then, if you can afford it, buy two good coats and two good jackets, since that's what you're seen in first.
• Supplement these investments with thirteen-button navy wool pants, cotton and velour pullovers, T-shirts, and cotton drawstring pants.
• Shoes and boots are some of the most important things you can have in your wardrobe. Spend money on styles like short pink boots cuffed at the top, brandy kidskin boots, ponyskin pumps—things that really set you off.
• All other shopping can be done from thrift shops and army surplus—here's where

you find your basics and special accessories, lots of bright belts, and jewelry.

The color, the quality, and the limited quantity of this wardrobe give you a luxurious style on a tight budget. Special accessories raise it from the rank of a working-woman's uniform.

You're always going to get the most out of your money by buying something really luxurious that makes you feel fantastic, wearing it to death, and paying absolutely rock bottom for the cheap things you can get away with. Draw the line at quality; don't skimp on the classics. And in ten years, who knows? You might even have an air of shabby gentility! Classics are clothes that last.

Soft wool sweaters over a loose classic skirt, silk shirt with the collar up, good boots . . . comfy classics.

ACCESSORIES

Sink your money into a very good pair of **boots.** Expensive European boots are a consistent favorite among snappy dressers who spend their money sparingly but buy things that last. You'll often find a pair of four-year-old St. Laurent boots making a very cheap turnout look terribly chic. It's not because they bear the name St. Laurent, though he does have a first-rate sense of classic design. It's because they're made in a European

A favorite felt hat with the perfect, small gold and enamel earrings are both classic investments.

artisan tradition with good lasts, hand finishing, the best leathers, and sumptuous colors.

Boots not only look good, they feel good. How far and how fast can you walk in a pair of high-heeled pumps? Boots look just as good, and you can really walk your heart out in them. The money you save on cabs and buses will pay for the next pair. But a European last is uncomfortable for some American feet, so never talk yourself into a pair of good boots unless they fit perfectly. A seamstress can do nothing about this particular problem!

Although it's perfectly sensible to buy black or brown, some girls go out and find just one pair of the very best boots in colors like gray, red, green, or burgundy. They figure it looks like you have lots more at home. So if acid green cheers you up, why not acid green?

Well dressed? Look down. Expensive boots and expensive shoes are worth saving up for. Not because of a designer label but because one good pair is the basis for a pared down, solid classic wardrobe. They age well, too.

The best quality, quietly conservative **men's shoes** can be found in the Brooks Brothers catalog. Peal & Company and the "Brooks English" line have wingtips with very thin soles, not those thick Big Mac numbers most guys walk around on, as well as simple oxfords and rakish tassel loafers. If you want to head for the very best, Lobb Bootmaker's representative takes orders in the spring and fall at a shop called Everall Brothers in New York.

Belts are worth an investment, since they will last a lifetime. A silver belt looks spectacular with anything from a tweed skirt to a pair of skintight leather jeans. Be sure any "investment belt" can fit in both places, at the waist or hip. You can occasionally find antique silver belts from Turkey at street markets and obscure shops, but they usually wend their way to the more pricey boutiques and antique stores. If you buy one of the large silver belts sold by weight, the heavier the better. (You can always hock it.) If you don't like silver, keep your eyes open for that unique, one-of-a-kind belt that looks as if it had always belonged to you, and buy it on the spot.

A good basic leather belt, totally simple, can be worn with interchangeable buckles. The buckles can be your personal trademarks. For about $25 you can buy a fine lizard belt from Tony Lama at a western

The ultimate in custom— made shoes are these now forbidden, handmade, crocodile tasseled loafers worn by Richard Merkin.

Find jewelry you'll keep a lifetime at auctions at Parke-Bernet. Ask to be listed for catalogues, and bid by mail.

store to wear with a big oval silver-and-gold rodeo belt buckle. Steer clear of imitation-antique, imitation-brass buckles, because there are just too many of them around.

A concho belt in silver, turquoise, and worn brown leather is a collector's item, a good investment now that they are no longer at the height of fashion. If you prefer to wear your art around your waist rather than on a wall, here's your chance.

Real jewelry adds a quiet little touch of elegance. Perhaps the most beautiful and inexpensive gold jewelry comes from Thailand—simple, tiny gold chains bought by the ounce, closed by a hand-soldered S. A plain gold chain looks perfect at wrist, waist, finger, or neck. Smooth hoops in pierced ears last a lifetime, and a gold band is almost nicer than a diamond. Gold can always be sold or bartered—it's much better than dollars.

If you wear a **watch,** you'll probably be seeing more of that than anything else you own. The nicest watches seem to be the most simple, not too tiny and "feminine," but something with a readable face and the best-quality brown or black leather band you can afford.

Today, the size of your **bag** seems to matter more than variety or expense. It used to be that you could always spot a "lady" by her shoes and purse. But now many of us are walking around in sneakers with portable offices in our purses—address book, note pad, appointment calendar, magazines, some letters, bills, makeup, Instamatic, small electronic calculator, checkbook, and wallet. With all this stuff to cart around, size becomes the primary consideration. The best place to find a sturdy leather or canvas bag is in the luggage department, in sporting goods stores, or at prestigious old-line leathergoods shops like Crouch & Fitz-

If you must wear a watch, choose one carefully so it will blend with all of your clothes and still be functional.

gerald in New York. A leather bag from a department store is going to cost too much: a simple legal-pad-sized shoulder bag is now up to $140, and the Hermès leather shoulder bag is a staggering $600 with tax.

If you can't afford a leather bag, it's awfully luxurious to use a leather-lined canvas bag, if you can find one. Some sly women-about-town buy the $30 Danish schoolbag by mail from Chocolate Soup in

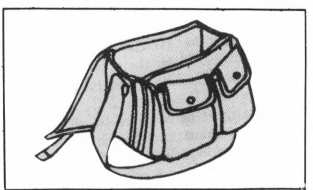

The Danish Souperbag has pockets for everything!

New York and sink the rest of their money into one beautiful, obviously expensive leather accessory like an address book or small monogramed diary from a place like Mark Cross. Whether you choose leather or canvas, it's always nice to have a clutch purse slipped inside for pared-down situations, like a business lunch at a good restaurant.

CLOTHES CLASSICS

Old etiquette books used to list the minimum wardrobe an impoverished gentleman of quality might collect. It is a system of dressing where less is more . . . of necessity! Transposing the rules for a man's wardrobe to a woman's can give you a fresh approach for a well-thought-out closet.

Three or four suits: a brown one, a gray pinstripe, a tweed or tan gabardine, and, in hot climates, a summer seersucker or white linen.

Jackets: One navy blazer and one brownish tweed sport coat.

Two or three pair of pants: gray flannel, beige whipcord, and perhaps white flannel for eccentricity's sake.

Three pair of shoes: brown single-sole wingtips, brown tassel loafers, and perfectly plain black oxfords.

A woman organizing her wardrobe on this minimalist principle would substitute a skirt here and a riding jacket there. Think of the ease with which you could dress. There would be absolutely no room to make a mistake (unless something didn't get back from the cleaner's in time for you to get to work in the morning!). Think of the beautiful, uncommon effect of such understated elegance—especially when mixed in with a few pair of Levi's and shiny boots. A couple of things from the classics lend presence and weight to all the clothes in your closet.

Before we run through some of the classic investments you might want to make, we offer a word of warning: In buying tailored clothes, steer clear of foppish effects like flapped and buttoned pockets, patch

Francois de Menil blends a classic St. Laurent blazer, a silk shirt, Levi's jeans and Lucchese boots from Texas.

pockets, contrasting-color overstitching on lapels, snazzy buttons, inverted pleats, epaulets, and gewgaws of all descriptions. You're going for well-tailored, expensive clothes that will not call attention to themselves and will not look out of fashion in six to eight years. Try to find an old-line conservative tailor whose judgment you can trust. Look at old pictures in movie books and magazines—there really are timeless looks that you can step right into today.

The **blazer** is one of the most elegant yet congenial designs from the classical repertoire. Navy blue is the traditional color; the cut is usually double breasted. If you have a blazer tailor made, it can be lengthened and shortened, made boxier or more shapely, according to the feel of the times. The blazer is ageless.

A black velvet blazer or lush green smoking jacket has become a dinner party classic. Wear it with cowboy boots, jeans, and an old belt. Put a flower at the lapel (gardenias waft deliciously as you walk down the street), put a wisp of silk at the neck or, if

Most classic wardrobes include a calf-length cape, a well fitted wool riding jacket and an all purpose raincoat. Left: Captain Bogart rides the waves in a timeless, navy wool crewneck sweater.

you can't get a fresh flower, make yourself a cluster of satin lingerie flowers from the twenties. And blaze.

If you must have a **suit,** it's best to get one that can go a million different ways—the jacket with jeans, the slacks with shirts and Shetlands. The owner of a men's boutique in New York suggests that a dark blue suit with a vest is the absolute minimum a man can have in his closet (along with a pair of Levi's, a drip-dry shirt, and a silk shirt). Another designer likes a navy serge suit backed up with a chalk pinstripe and a gray flannel—all paired with shirts of the same tone. A Prince of Wales glen plaid suit is the height of daytime elegance but trousers can't live a double life as easily as gray flannel or blue serge, but that's the price you pay for the sublime! Lauren Bacall wears a black, man's tailored suit with a polka-dot silk hankie and fuschia stitching on the lapel buttonhole.

You can dress a **riding jacket** up or down, over a Shetland sweater and jeans, or with a silk shirt and luscious brown velvet skirt.

George Stavrinos

Italy's Giorgio Armani: designs of subtle, refined simplicity brushed with the most elegant colors .

Dietrich's mysterious sexuality changed the tailored look.

The psychology of a riding jacket is fascinating, especially if it has a worldly patina. It seems to demand a stance of being in command, a certain swagger and controlled elegance . . . pure attitude. If it's difficult to find a riding jacket in your area, you can order from one of the riding stores in New York that stock English and French imports, and have it tailored once it arrives.

A good pair of pure wool **slacks** will last years. If you can't afford to have them custom-tailored, you can order something called made-to-measure, put together from a combination of existing patterns. Or you can order by mail from Brooks, Chipp, or Press. Women can find well-cut slacks in boutiques and good department stores. Gray is a good color if you can only afford one pair, as is beige gabardine. Navy blue wool has a very sober and bracing elegance and can take you anywhere. The best cut is very conservative, with small pleats and straight legs. If they start to get shiny, they can be deshined by a special cleaning process listed in the back of this book. Tailor-made slacks

cost little more than very good ones in department stores. If you find the right tailor, you can get them for $50–$80, and have everything exactly as you like it—pockets, watch pocket, cuffs, pleats, belt loops, zipper or button fly.

A **cape** is a necessary accoutrement for swirly, dramatic people. Look for a fluid, loose, ample fabric you can whoosh around in, drape over your arm, or throw over a shoulder like a scarf for the body. The black wool Spanish cape with its high collar is a good buy. The full-length wool Inverness cape from Scotland is especially dashing. And plain old cashmere makes the softest cape of all.

To wrap up the classics in the middle of

Never go anywhere without a trench coat. This is St. Laurent's; Burberry or Brooks Brothers are comparable.

a downpour, try a British **trench coat.** The Burberry is more than a raincoat—it can serve as a top layer year round, over a thick sweater in winter and a thin T-shirt in summer showers. The trench coat design is timeless, with its epaulets, knotted belt, slash pockets, and raglan sleeves.

We talk a lot about the **silk shirt.** A good one is hard to find. Some people dislike silk because it tends to feel clammy if you perspire. The secret to wearing a silk shirt is to buy it very loose, so that it is not cut in tightly under the armpits. Then perspiration is able to evaporate off your body and won't stain the armpit. The other problem with silk is that it takes an incredible beating at the cleaners. So the other secret to wearing a silk shirt is learning to wash it gently by hand in lukewarm water and then have it pressed at the cleaner's. Once you master the care and feeding of a silk shirt, there is nothing that will look so luxurious, wear so beautifully, and feel so incredible. Silk picks up everything you own, including your spirits.

Yves St. Laurent makes ample silk shirts in a wide variety of colors. One of his crepe de Chine shirts has full sleeves, a sheared back and front, a narrow collar band, and a front placket. It is soft and loose; the look is elegant lassitude. Tuck it in as a blouson, wear it out as an overshirt, wrap it with a wide leather belt, or knot it over a swirling skirt. Or wear one traditional shirt over another and layer the collars like the petals of a flower.

You can often find a better shirt in the men's line—the cut is bigger, the tails are longer, the stitching is closer. Turnbull & Asser of London will make them up in any shape you prefer for around $125, or in the very finest cotton for less. If you're not ready to spring a week's wages for a shirt, send for samples of the beautiful $10-a-yard crepe de Chine at Oriental Silk in Los Angeles and ask a seamstress to copy a friend's shirt. Or, again, you could be patient and do very well at a half-price sale. Silk shirts that have faded where they've been folded sometimes sell for $25 at St. Laurent (25 percent of their original price) but they need to be dyed a dark color or worn under

A classic silk tunic-length shirt by Pinky & Dianne, sleeves pushed up for a casual look.

a sweater so just the collars and cuffs show.

Richard Merkin dresses only in tailored clothes and thinks they are, indeed, heaven incarnate. Every morning Richard gets up in his apartment on New York's West Side, pulls on a battered old gray sweatsuit, and jogs through Riverside Park. When he gets back, he changes into his work clothes and goes into his painter's studio until three in the afternoon. Then, Richard turns toward his vast, overflowing closet and chooses the suit, tie, shirt, collar, suspenders, socks, and shoes for his tailor-made composition of the day. Richard Merkin, artist, becomes Richard Merkin, noted dandy, a man fascinated by dress, and especially by the aristocratic British tailoring which he affects to an extreme. Once you read and absorb Richard Merkin's views, you should be able to talk to any British tailor with ease. Tailor-made clothes are nothing more or less than a collaboration between you and the tailor; part fabric, part psychology. Here's what happens when a man (or woman, for that matter) develops a craving for The Real Thing.

48 | **Richard Merkin's classic dinner jacket is highlighted by a lavender carnation and a slick shoeshine.**

"I started having clothes made for me in the sixties, when my first show of paintings sold out in Boston. Before that I couldn't afford it! My suits from 1964 look as new as a suit I would have made today. But ten years ago, you could get a really good custom suit for $190 . . . now a good custom suit is upwards of $380.

"George Frazier was the most elegant man I've ever known, a columnist and journalist who wrote for *Esquire* and the Boston *Globe*. He didn't have very much clothing, but everything he had was impeccable. There was no room for any mistake. And it wasn't self-conscious, it was at one with him. Every so often I used to wear both a flower and a handkerchief, and George always chided me for it. He said it was disturbing to have put the two things together. He was right. It's just a spot of color that accents a whole totality. And it shouldn't be two spots.

"I like the idea of being able to take a classical form and punctuate it with invention so that you come up with something like a new color combination, or just using an unexpected collar with a suit. Most guys who were concerned dressers in the twenties wore flowers in their lapel. People come up to me and say, 'Where did you get that flower?' It's just a carnation. But the point of it is the concern, of course. I mean, a flower is really beautiful, it's very perfect . . . a beautiful flower and a good shoeshine. Nowadays most ready-made suits have no buttonhole. How sad.

"George Frazier always said, 'Wanna know if a guy is well-dressed? Look down.' The greatest degeneration of any particular garment is shoes. The nicest shoes you can find are those old Brooks Brothers brown ones. Outside of dancing pumps, they're the most elegant. I wear dancing pumps a lot in the summer when I'm not wearing socks. And I love tassel loafers.

"I think we live in a time when people are superficially more interested in dress than they ever have been. People today want approval for the way they dress, which is the kiss of death. You really can't 'do your own thing' unless you know who you are. I think there's a very delicate kind of merger between your clothes and your personality, a give and take between who you are and what you're wearing. When I get dressed, I do become a little bit more severe, more decisive. Actually, I think the most fashionable dressers are the nonfash-

Mr. Merkin, a perfectionist in his attire, likes to accent his grey pinstripe double-breasted suit with a British bowler and butter cotton gloves.

David Croland bought his one dollar tuxedo in a thrift shop, had it recut twice and is determined to have it copied if it doesn't hold up for another five years.

ionable dressers. Style really has to do with being able to perceive what's best for you; taking care to analyze just the way something really looks. For instance, a really big tie doesn't look good on everybody. I can't stand shirts with crippling patterns. You have to be very careful about things like lapels, which can get too big and fall into caricature and trendiness.

"The really great dandies devoted a major section of their life to dressing. Certainly in Beau Brummell's case it didn't lead to ostentation. It led to dressing that was perfect, just absolutely perfect, nothing off, not a hair!

"Obviously, that takes a lot of concern and a lot of time. If you need two hours to dress in the morning and you have to be at work at nine, then you have to get up at seven. Is that approaching insanity? No, it's approaching perfection, but then perfection is just a stone's throw away from insanity.

"I don't understand the passion for informality, the contemporary loathing for discipline. There's an absolute fetish these days about being comfortable, being loose. But I rather like the idea of a starched collar.

It's not as comfortable as an open-neck shirt . . . but it's beautiful looking! Why not put up with a little discomfort to achieve a more significant effect?

"When I say somebody dresses well, I mean cohesively. It doesn't mean just like me. For instance, I'm a fight fan and I've seen some pimp types who were fabulously dressed! Those guys really know what their *body* looks like.

"I'm terribly contrary, and if something becomes popular, it generally gets ruined, and I'll give it up like that! I never wear jeans. And I don't like costume, putting things together for an effect which may not be beautiful and may not have anything to do with your life. I like things that are ordered, the same kind of order I look for in a painting or in a supper or in a girlfriend or in a car . . . a blend of the function and the form of it.

"Art is exactly as important to me as the way I dress. When I choose a tie and a shirt in the morning it's no less important to me than going in and making a picture. It's the same.

"But I am an artist, so I really hate it when I buy a shirt and the guy says 'Would you like a tie to go with that?' It's the 'go with' syndrome. And if somebody puts his name on something, I don't buy it. I'll wear a tailor's name, but a designer's? Any person is a unique totality, and what does St. Laurent know about where I grew up and what I think?

"Unless something is made absolutely right, it bothers me, so I spend the extra money. But if I didn't have any money, I'd much rather go to a thrift shop and find some old English suit or jacket and bring it to a tailor than go buy something off the rack in a department store.

"You see, most people mistrust any kind of classical values or verities. I think there are certain articles of clothing that are absolutely the most impeccable: the summer Panama hat, a black satin tie with a clean knot, a navy blue blazer, the pink Brooks button-down, a double-breasted Chesterfield with a black velvet collar. I mean, all these things are just absolutely the *zenith* of gorgeousness. All you have to do is buy them! There it is!"

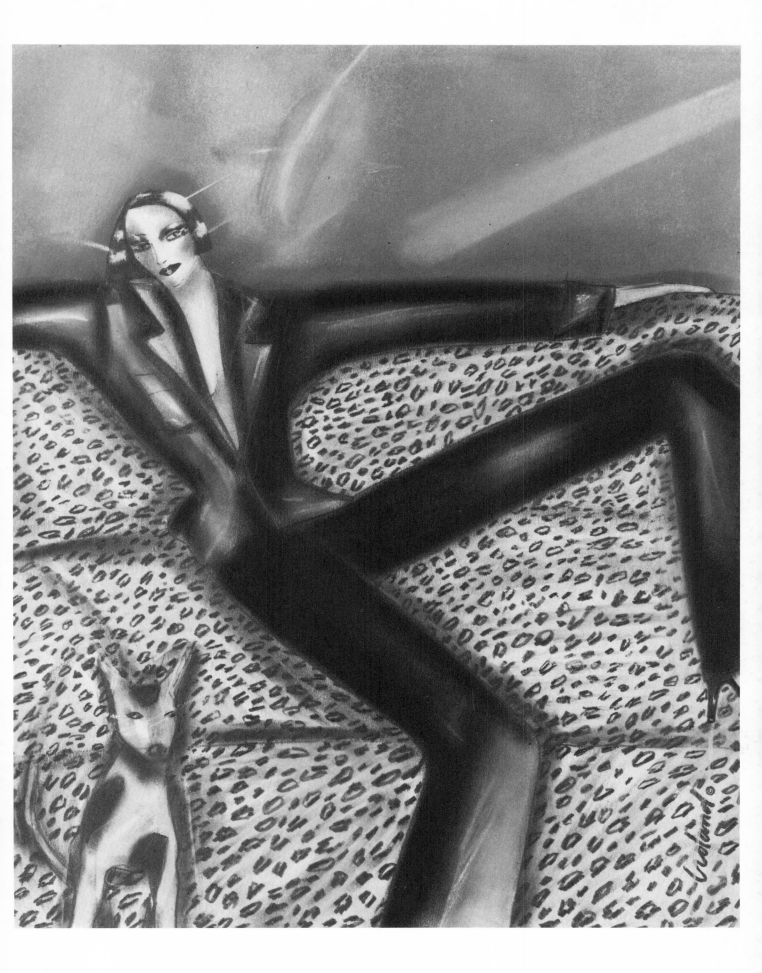

DIANA VREELAND

Eccentric Elegance from the World of Vogue

For more than thirty-five years, Diana Vreeland has been a leading figure in the international world of fashion, first at Harper's Bazaar and then as editor-in-chief at Vogue. Since October 1972 Mrs. Vreeland has been Special Consultant to the Costume Institute at the Metropolitan Museum of Art in New York. The world she has experienced ranges from the extravagances of the twenties in Paris to the creation of the

The super-pros at the Metropolitan's Costume Institute.

Beautiful People, a mix of society and fashion, in the sixties. Called "Empress Vreeland" in some papers, Mrs. Vreeland has completed her autobiography that is sure to intrigue fashion insiders.

A woman of great charisma and originality, Diana Vreeland speaks her mind about style, the importance of a fit body, and an element she still exudes in her mid-seventies, energy.

"I think everything is habit. Everything builds on itself. Energy builds on energy like love builds on love. Everything intensifies itself. This is habit. Energy and love are good habits, sometimes there are bad habits. Stimulation is happy energy. Then the energy produces itself and your excitement about whatever is going on.

"I think it's a very difficult moment to write a book on fashion. The first thing a girl's got to do is to keep herself together physically with any small amount of money she's got. However she does it, that comes before anything. This is a very vital moment. You have to be very healthy today—your skin, your eyes, your everything.

"Basically, people only look well if they have a very, very good foundation. You know what that means? You can't cover anything up with paint and powder. But I am tired of the natural look. I am fed up to the teeth. God Almighty, some of the girls who come into my office. Oh, how they look! For what is all this natural look? It must be for them, it certainly can't mean

Mrs. Vreeland's classic winter uniform: three black cashmere sweaters rotated with three black Givenchy skirts.

anything to anyone else. I am mad about artificial appearances beautifully done—the gilded lily is irresistible.

"The natural look is too colorless. Don't forget that the white person is not beautiful. Pale skin is not beautiful. It's very rare you see extraordinarily clear white skin. It's usually sallow. We are uneven owing to the many mixtures of bloods. So we've got to build ourselves up to something.

"You have to start with your face and hair and your body. Forget clothes until you've got these basics straight. Once you've got that in hand (if you're young you can do it very quickly), then you get with the clothes. I think clothes come second. Clothes are decor and you've got to have something to put them on. I'm not talking about expensive clothes. I don't see why clothes should be expensive. But don't forget I am talking about a girl with everything absolutely as best as she can do it . . . her hair, her eyes, her strength, her walk, her expression, everything. She's totally with it. That comes before clothes. Men the same. And for children too, but they have it naturally.

"First, I'd put money into shoes. No variety, just something I could wear with everything. Marvelous shoes and boots. Whatever it is you wear, I think shoes are terribly important. My shoe, that strap shoe, I had made again and again for about thirty years. Now I have pumps and boots made exactly as I want them.

"Style is everything. Style is the most important word. I think we've lost some of the sense of what 'fashion' means. But I'll tell you why I don't think fashion is over. First, I don't think any of us know now what we're talking about when we say fashion. If you mean dictatorship of fashion, no one at the moment has anything to dictate. But once they do, we'll be very pleased and excited to hear it. Fashion is a rhythm controlled by the economic and social conditions of the times, and neither our social nor economic condition is very good. But I do think that clothes today are very pretty. There is a repose, a charm about the new clothes.

"I believe I just really like clothes. Peo-

ple want to be a little too deep about the whole thing. But I think all charming women will always have a sense of the refined, a sense of delight, and a sense of themselves. I don't envision a somber world. One likes certain things. For instance, I never thought the style of the thirties was remotely interesting, and I was living in a full world in those days. There

was no war, there was no visible depression in Europe, and Paris was absolutely remarkable. The clothes were beautifully composed and shown but they were never, to me, really interesting. I don't understand today's fascination with the clothes of the thirties. If you only knew how really weak they were after the clothes of the twenties.

"Today, I suppose Pucci and Gucci is good because it stimulates people toward a status symbol, but it keeps people apart. When I was in Beverly Hills I went down Wilshire Boulevard on a Saturday afternoon and saw crowds of cars and people. Usually there are never many people—after all, it's not a big city. And I said to my son, who was driving, 'Oh God, I hope it isn't an accident!' And he said, 'Good God no,

Diana Vreeland visits Kyoto with the Couture Show from the Met: Do it right, do it big, give it class! 55

that's just Saturday afternoon at Gucci's.' I just couldn't believe what I saw. All these men bring in girls that want to shop. That's all they want. At the end of the week it's 'Baby, I'll take you to Gucci if you're good.' This makes a lot of people happy, so put it down as good for business.

"You need a sense of humor in fashion, you have to see where you are. For instance, I've never tried wearing synthetics. It just never came my way. But I do remember one experience very well. I was motoring up to Maine for the weekend. I went to Brooks Brothers and bought myself a Dacron shirt, the copy of the men's pale blue button-down shirt—all the English and Europeans who came over bought them by the dozen and said they were marvelous.

"We got through Boston and it was terribly hot . . . we were in a traffic jam and we couldn't move. And you know, I thought I was in a fire! I had to open the shirt completely, I had to get out of it, and my husband said, 'In the name of God, what are you doing!' But I really and truly was in flames locked in this synthetic thing.

"I wouldn't have felt a chemical fire if I had been wearing pure cotton. It just would have been damned hot. But this was what I call an experience. Synthetics, however, have simplified the life of all of us. I suppose polyesters and so on are marvelous. They make clothes stand up and out and all that, which is great . . . for people who like it.

"It's been very curious, moving from a magazine to a museum, because now there are no daily deadlines. But all of the shows I've worked on have been revelations. You think of the idea, and then of course, panic. Is it a good idea? Will it charm, pull and amuse the imagination? Can I pull it off? You don't know until you really work at it. But each show has been so marvelously revealing and wonderful. As you unpack the clothes coming from this museum and that, from Rome and Madrid, you look at them and you're so glad they're beautiful. It is never a letdown, never. It's always been just right! Now we have taken the couture show to the Modern Museum in Kyoto. It's the first time an Eastern museum has ever asked for a collection of European clothes.

"When I go through the Costume Institute at the Metropolitan Museum, one thing is more beautiful than the next, so well arranged, so well shown. Everything breathes, everything is free . . . they're alive, these clothes. You don't know how beautiful it is!

"Last year I used some Schiaparelli clothes from the thirties and we were very short of original hats. So we found some Southern Russian hats of the nineteenth century, all in solid silver embroidery, more or less the same shape, just like 'Schiap' used to make. I knew her collection well and these were absolutely suitable. It wasn't cheating in any way. You don't notice these things. You just see the effect and they're exactly correct.

"And for the Hollywood clothes exhibition, this dear gentleman asked, 'Would you be interested in Mary Pickford's curls?' He keeps them in a Baggie and I said, 'Where in the name of God did you get them?' He said, 'But she sent them to us for the Los Angeles Historical Museum.' Isn't that marvelous? After all, in all the world, those curls were the most special, just perfect . . . 'America's Sweetheart,' the first star, everything!

"In the beautiful gown from **The Bride Wore Red**, Elizabeth Lawrence, who works on all the costumes, noticed that the bugle beads are all shaded as it fits the body. It's fantastic—the highest, highest couture refinement. It's total. I told a French couturier, 'You'll never find better-made clothes than these Hollywood outfits in any Paris workroom in the last forty years,' which is as far back as I can go. The great thing that went out across the studios from Louis B. Mayer when a new movie was being made in Hollywood was, 'Do it right. Do it big. Give it class!'

"Those Hollywood designers knew how to dream up extraordinary clothes and dress beautiful women. You can always find great artisans. You can always get quality if you demand it.

"And what happens in five or ten years? Who's worrying? Every year I'm told it's the last Ball in Venice. All my life, the last Ball. But I've had a long life and gone to a hell of a lot of Balls. And life goes on very much the same."

YVES St. LAURENT

Sticking with the Classics

Yves St. Laurent is the top designer of our age. He is French, or rather Parisian: an elegant, understated perfectionist who makes it all look very easy, lazy, languid—and very sensual. His clothes for men and women are very special, very contemporary, but they always remain in style.

At forty-two, St. Laurent is still youthful. He has a strangely confident shyness, as if his slight smile is about to be captured by a flashbulb. After becoming the star designer of the House of Dior at twenty-one, he was drafted into the French Army, suffered a nervous breakdown, and came back to start his own couture house. St. Laurent is now part of a conglomerate, Lanvin-Charles of the Ritz, which backs his perfume. He himself has couture, jewelry, fabric, Rive Gauche ready-to-wear, accessories, perfume, and men's wear ventures. American retailers say, "St. Laurent is like money in the bank."

"It is good for me to come here, to New York. It is very exciting. The United States is going through the crisis we had in France after May 1968, like the consequence of the riots. Perhaps because they're not accustomed to this kind of crisis, this kind of depression, Americans are much more upset than in Paris, saying that life must change, that new things must come. On the street, I see only blue jeans. . . . This is the first time I have been in the United States when there is so little involvement in the fashion sphere. Perhaps it is because blue jeans give more confidence.

"This crisis, this depression, of course influences me in some way. More and more I believe in well-made, basic clothes with no 'fashion' that last many years without transformation—exactly like a blue jean. 'Classic' seems to be an old-fashioned word, but I think the contrary. A blue jean is a classic and I don't think it's old. I believe in basics,

LULU JOYEUSE   LULU TRISTE   LULU LUXE   Qu'on brûle tout so le qu'on brûle tout do mi sol fa   LULU NERONE   LULU BATMAN   LULU DE BAR   LULU JUST A WOMAN   Vilaine LULU MIDI-MINUIT

a wardrobe for a woman that is like a man's—exactly like a blue jean—pants, jacket, raincoat, not similar in details, but in mind. But if an amusing thing happens in fashion, why not try . . . but I don't like too much 'fashion.' Things must have a direction, a continuity.

"Now people are aware of their individuality more and more. To have style you must believe in yourself.

"The men's designs for St. Laurent Rive Gauche are exactly the same here as in France. I don't believe in special things for one country or another. Fashion is the same more and more. And more and more I don't think about the age of the woman or the man. There is no age to wear my clothes. They are basic. It is important to be yourself, not to want to look younger.

"Clothes are things that must last a lot of years without transformation. I like pure fabrics—cotton, silk, wool. I am unable to work with synthetics. Mixtures, yes, but synthetics have a contrary reaction for the body. I don't even like working with mixes, but what can we do? The time is coming in the world when a silk shirt will be a treasure.

"I find that prices are really too high. It's a question of the materials being so expensive. Everything is made in France. There are no workmanship problems, but to reduce prices I think the only thing to do is to be more and more specialized in a kind of clothes. Again, classics.

"The Paris woman in the past one or two years has been very exciting in fashion. Perhaps it was not so before. Recently Paris has taken a new vitality, new shape. There is a new woman with more sense of quality and refinement in life. A mixture of serious and giggle, a good balance in life for me. But the American woman has been the first image of the modern woman. It is a good experience to come here. In Paris perhaps, not to be pejorative, but because of all the continental traditions, they dress more seriously. France is full of traditions.

"A woman can feel very sexy in a chemise, as she can feel very sexy in jeans. It depends on the person. If she thinks she isn't sexy, she will not be sexy."

SUITE - LES VILAINES - LES LULUS -

LULU GOLDONI

LULU GIRONDE

Vilaine Lulu ROUSSE

LULUZIZI

Vilaine Lulu de SCALA

Vilaine Lulu Debuza

LULU HENNIN

LULU ECCLÉSIASTIQUE

LULU JOYEUSE

LULU TRISTE

LULU LOLITA

Vilaine Lulu d'un certain genre

VILAINE LULU DE SAINT-PHALL

LULU MATRONE

Vilaine Lulu de Médicis et vilaine Galigaï

VILAINE LULU MITEUSE

LE GRAND MÉCHANT LOUP EST EN RETARD

LULU CHAPERON ROUGE

LULU PEAU D'ÂNE

St. Laurent's cartoons of his mischievous little French character called Lulu.

SECOND-STRING CLASSICS

IVY LEAGUE AND WESTERN

Now that we've taken you through the never-never land of high finance and international tailoring, we want to tell you that it's all right: You don't have to spend all that money. If you want to look rumpled and tweedy without all the formality and expense of custom-made clothes and silk shirts, you can turn to the Ivy League look. Or if you want to look like the quintessential American, you can turn to Western classics.

THE IVY LEAGUE LOOK

Brooks Brothers has been called the Chanel of men's wear for sticking with the simplest designs year after year until they have become as classic and recognizable as a Chanel suit. The Brooks style provides a gently wrinkled old-money look in a range of subtle colors. These are the clothes you see on those mythic couples walking the deserted beach of Martha's Vineyard in early

The classic Brooks Brothers Ivy League casuals—stripes, Bermuda shorts and white bucks.

Parisian Ivy Leaguer in a reversible poplin raincoat.

spring, sipping a summer drink in Southampton, sitting on the terrace of the Ivy Club after a Princeton game, or browsing for antiques at a Chicago auction gallery. It is a very precise way of dressing, almost like an unwritten code, and one item of clothing seems to require the corresponding item. So although you can mix a Brooks look with jeans, dressing it down, you would drive classicists crazy by wearing Brooks

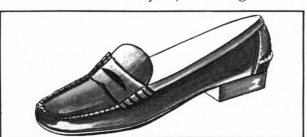

slacks with a shiny red ciré motorcycle jacket. But that's just what you should do if you feel like it.

The Ivy League look for summer runs something like this.

Shirt: An English cotton lisle polo shirt by Solly for the guy, a simple French cotton T-shirt for the girl. A pale blue, pink, or yellow button-down shirt under a light cable-knit sweater for both on cooler evenings.

Wear the shirt or T-shirt with yellow, tomato, or beige chino straight-legged pants, midwale corduroy slacks (perhaps in a bright color), corduroy jeans, or blue jeans. Belt the pants with solid-color webbing finished with leather closings.

On the feet: Weejun loafers or Top-Siders worn without socks.

When it gets chillier, the Ivy League dresser pulls a Shetland sweater or off-white Irish fisherman's knit over the shirt, with cords or jeans. The guy tops this off with an old tweed sport jacket that is meant to look as if it was handed down from his father (but could just as well have come from the local thrift shop). The girl pulls on an old tweed riding jacket or single-breasted blazer. In blustery weather, the old worn

beige gabardine raincoat with reversible wool hounds-tooth check makes its appearance. These seasonal fashion changes are as dependable as the coming of autumn.

A modification of the Brooks look can be really stunning on a pretty girl. For instance, you could collect a few Brooks V-neck cashmere and wool sweaters in pale pastels and wear them big and baggy over tight Lee jeans and a pair of high-heeled, gray St. Laurent boots. Add some plain gold chains here and there and you have a look both boyish and sophisticated.

The rules of dressing in Ivy League classics can be almost as stiff and demanding as those of the custom-made universe. But this just gives you all the more room for innovation and invention within the basic form. Rules are made to be broken.

COWBOY CLASSICS

Cowboy clothes were once designed for survival on the range, but now they're our most popular home-grown classic. "Western clothes were originally survival clothes," wrote Jon Carroll in *Rags* magazine, "and

The essence of rodeo tailoring: country sequins.

Brooks Brothers supplies the Shetland sweater and cotton shirt; Lauren Hutton supplies the sneakers and smile.

these elementary jeans, according to *Rags*, "tucked into the tops of heavy leather boots. A red flannel shirt was worn outside the trousers and gathered round the waist with a scarf of Chinese silk or a leather belt, or both, with a holster for a heavy Colt revolver. And any sort of hat . . . except the stovepipe beaver. They didn't want any class symbols out on the Great Frontier."

The custom-made leather jeans of today may not be class symbols, but they sure look classy. Those of us who bought them five years ago in the "latest" bell-bottomed style made a big mistake. The leather is still in great shape, but that hip-slung flared-leg fashion just doesn't look right today. The safest way to order leather jeans is as an exact copy of whatever jeans you've been wearing since you first played cowboys and Indians. The best leather jeans (often costing over $100) are so sturdy they can be pummeled, scrubbed, and stomped in the bathtub. You save on those exorbitant cleaning bills.

Another staple in the Western repertoire is the cowboy shirt. It's cut tight to the body (so it doesn't flap while you're riding),

First class examples of "rodeo tailoring," both by Nudie of Hollywood. Right: Francois de Menil wears a conservative maroon and beige wool garbardine shirt tailored to fit the body. Above: a peach of a suit from one of Nudie's old catalogues. Add a buckskin skirt . . . that's cowgirl heaven.

their increasing relevance to our lives, along with the increasing relevance of the social and moral systems they symbolize, may say something about how close to the edge of the cliff of civilization we are."

Levi-Strauss jeans, as we've mentioned, are all-time classics. They began during the Gold Rush as sturdy trousers made of sailcloth, riveted with copper. The Americans and Europeans who headed west wore

Below: Cowboy Boots come in a dizzying array of colors, leathers and stitchings. What makes them a great investment is their rugged nature and timeless style.

yoked across the back and front, snapped on the sleeves and down the front, and flapped and snapped on the breast pockets. These shirts are especially handsome in plaids, ginghams, and solid colors, and take a bow tie or neck scarf with panache.

If you want conservative cowboy clothes, you can have them tailor-made by a "rodeo" tailor. We have seen beautiful wool gabardine shirts with contrasting yokes and white pearl snaps. One "formal" tailor-made jacket owned by a friend of ours has thirteen—count 'em, thirteen—buttons marching up the sleeve of the jacket, a sand and maroon gabardine trimmed with white piping on the yoke, patch pockets, and sleeves. It never fails to get a few conversations going during a stroll down Broadway. A really elegant way to wear these understated cowboy clothes is to put them together with jeans and a silk shirt for a party. It shows you care enough to make an extra effort to "dress," while letting you keep your own particular style of dress-up.

If you want even flashier cowboy clothes, send to Los Angeles for the catalog from Nudie the Rodeo Tailor. He does the rancher look as well as the gaudiest "parade class" around—electric colors, metallic trims, flashing fringe, sequins, and glittering jewels. If the Flying Burrito Brothers are your kind of rock group, Nudie's is your kind of store.

Cowboy boots are a well-heeled alternative to a pair of European "investment" boots. Although custom-made boots can easily run you up to $250, you can still find mail-order cowboy boots for under $100, custom-made to a drawing of your foot. The

prices are so reasonable because many Texas bootmakers use artisans over the border in Mexico. The design of the boot makes it good looking and sensible for the rider. The boot is shaped to give leverage in the saddle, the pointed toes get the arch into the stirrup fast, and the high heels catch the foot so you can't be dragged by the ankle. Genghis Khan and his Mongol warriors wore boots heeled with bright red to celebrate their fierce occupation and high status, but we can merrily outdo him. Joe Hall in El Paso

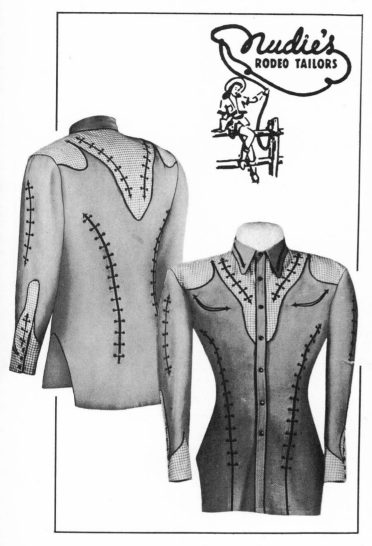

Today, just as in 1886, feathers and leathers have a classy look. Left: A timeless style, that fitted custom cut of a classic Western shirt.

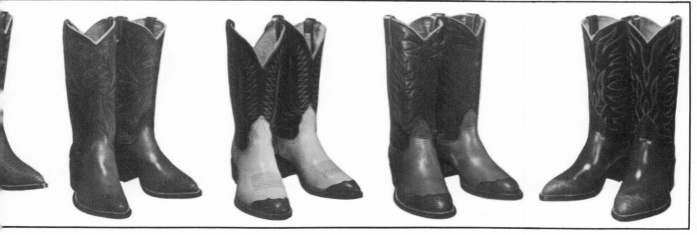

makes up boots in cowhide, veal, steerhide, calfskin, horsehide, kangaroo, boarhide, sharkskin, ostrich, elephant, and snakeskin, with bright colors to match. Some of his best customers are professional wrestlers, men who really know how to put on a show; the boots he creates for them are real show-boats.

Some Western boot connoisseurs think the most satisfying thing about their elaborately stitched and overlaid high-top boots is the fact that all that icing is never seen, except in the owner's closet. It's not exactly conspicuous consumption. But we think you should show them off. You can tuck jeans or jumpsuits into the tops of stovepipes. You can make a long skirt look different by wearing it with mid-calf boots, or alter the proportion of a big knee-length skirt with short boots. It takes a while to adjust to the look of it, but short or mid-calf boots look really new without being in the least bit nostalgic.

JEAN-PAUL GOUDE

Fashioning the Body Beautiful

Jean-Paul Goude is an artist and art director who lives in a combined working and living space high above Union Square in Manhattan. He grew up in Paris with a French father and an American mother, and now lives in New York dreaming up ways to lengthen everyone's image, if not body. A meticulous artist, he combines photography and painting in such a personal and precise manner that you often cannot tell if you are seeing a picture or an illustration. Jean-Paul carries his personal brand of estheticism into his daily life and personal movie making.

"I've always art-directed my appearance. Naked, I have short legs. When I was a kid, I was doing men's fashion illustrations for Le Printemps department store in Paris. I gradually realized that these drawings were actually a projection of how I wanted to look. On paper I was elegant, long legged, broad shouldered, slim, etc. One day I decided to make the fantasy real, so I visited John Lobb, the bootmaker in Paris. Being conservative, I wanted a traditional shoe with no high heel, so the only solution was to have lifts put in them. I was twenty then. I still go to Lobb's. Now I'm six feet tall!

"Lobb shoes can cost up to $600, even more. It's not expensive because you get to wear them for ten years at least. I like white bucks too, and sneakers, but only with lifts.

"The American men's wear look is summed up for me by Brooks Brothers. It's not what it used to be, but it's still good when not trying to be 'continental.'

"I used to wear 'high-water' pants; you know, tight pants too short so you can see your socks (like Lil' Abner) because I liked the look of the rhythm-and-blues singers who used to perform in the Olympia in Paris. (That was in 1965, long before I came to live in the United States.) They were country boys and had a special style about them. I guess they were just 'country,' but to me they had a great look. I tried to wear 'high-waters,' but one has to be built like those guys to make it work.

"If one is small, one is almost forced to wear tight-fitting clothes. (James Cagney used to; so did Adolphe Menjou, even Fred

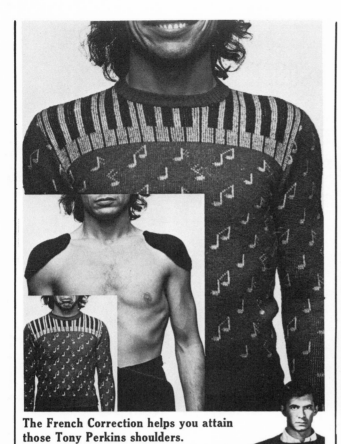

The French Correction helps you attain those Tony Perkins shoulders.
Add pads, glue them well and think tall. (No giggling!)

The sizzling energetic style of New York Puerto Ricans.

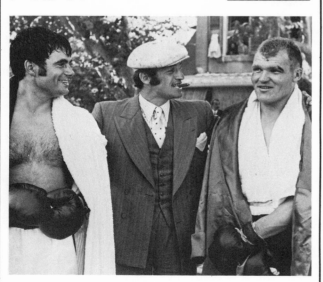

Good, better, best: noses in Jean-Paul's pantheon are OK on actor Jean Paul Belmondo, but the boxer at right has the truly perfect nose.

Astaire.) Did you ever see South American diplomats in the fifties, the ones who used to have their clothes made in Saville Row in London? They used to wear real tight jackets, rather wide trousers, and all the accessories; stiff collars, club ties, carna- tions in their lapel. They were a reduced version of the tall English dandies, only they had brown Indian faces and shiny black straight hair. They really looked great. Porfirio Rubirosa had that look, except he was tall.

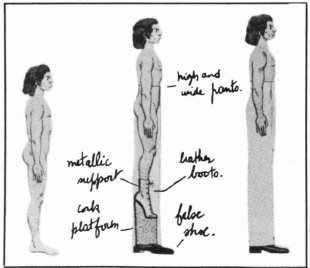

The French Correction II: To look like a fashion illustration, lengthen your lines with Jean-Paul's fantasy shoes. The normal shoe is buttressed with a towering cork platform, a metal support and lace-up boots and voilà, the designer's dream. (No wobbling.)

"In France, we have a certain idea of what Americans wear, and a lot of Frenchmen dress American when in fact Americans have stopped wearing these particular clothes, and are in turn wearing 'continental' clothes. Americans used to look great to us when they wore the Ivy League style. Now they wear Cardin suits which look like they are made of cardboard. It's a shame in a way, though I've seen some little French guys in their version of Brooks, and that can be sad too.

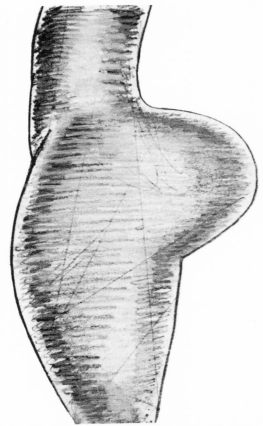

His ideal derrière is high, round, womanly and black.

"My tailor is Maurice Breslave. He used to be Eric Von Stroheim's tailor. Remember how great old Eric looked? Breslave still works for some of the best-dressed stars. He's the one who did those suits in the French movie Borsalino.

"Men are vain, but for some reason most of them think it's wrong to admit it. I guess they think it's not masculine.

"Tony Perkins used to look great in the late fifties before he started making films in Europe and tried to look French. He completely lost his style. He should go back to Brooks Brothers.

Sweatpants and white bucks with an impeccably tailored jacket, closed with an eccentric button at the neck.

The femme French Correction, or, Height is Pain.

"Don Robbie, St. Laurent's American men's wear designer, tried to capitalize on the way Puerto Rican teen-agers dress. He made them look like gangsters. I prefer to see those kids in their fifties thrift-shop clothes. They have such great taste and invention. It's funny, though, that it's the teen-age Puerto Ricans who have the taste. Through their influence Puerto Ricans have become the new ethnic stars.

"This reminds me of the 'Minets de L'-Étoile' when I was in my late teens. We were a whole gang hanging around the 'Drugstore' de L'Étoile in Paris. We wore blazers and flannel pants, trying to be very British. We came from the suburbs, not the elegant districts of Paris, but we looked more stylish than the rich kids. We were outdoing them with silk ties from polo clubs, monogramed shirts, cashmere scarves, and so on . . . I had a blazer made when I was about sixteen, and on the pocket was a gold embroidered emblem which I had copied from the golden eagle stamped on an American passport.

"My friends and I wanted to look like British clubmen and French race-horse owners. Consequently, I bought my first Rolls Royce when I was twenty-three, to complete the image; what I was doing actually was a softer European version of what black pimps are doing here. I never paid too much attention to physical characteristics at that time. I mean my face. But now, it's a different story. I always had a childish face because of my turned-up nose. The problem is, when you get a certain age and still have a kid's face you can easily look like an old

faggot. It's charming to have a kid's face when you're twenty-five, but I've just turned thirty-three, and I don't look so cute anymore. When I reach forty, I must have the 'face of a man,' a virile face. So I need a serious nose, not a kid's nose. If I had the nerve, I'd get a nose job. I'd have a boxer's nose done. But I don't trust plastic surgeons for myself because I'm too specific. I'd be scared they'd give me one of those obvious nose jobs. Too bad, I wouldn't mind looking like an ex-fighter when I'm forty.

"Mind you, I think plastic surgery and health spas will get so big they will be a threat to the garment industry. The better looking you are, the less clothes you need. In 1972, I started in Esquire the 'French correction,' in which I showed readers how to improve their appearance by wearing special shoes, shoulder pads in T-shirts, instant capped teeth, and so on.

"I still think it's a good idea, because people need advice before going into the hands of plastic surgeons who fancy themselves as modern versions of Leonardo Da Vinci, only they use a scalpel instead of a brush. I have seen so many rotten nose jobs done, I guess, by surgeons who could not draw. To become a truly great plastic surgeon, one should first win the 'Prix De Rome' in sculpture, then go into the medical profession.

"Sports are great to watch, not for the sport itself but for the way athletes move. I don't care much for ballet, but I've always liked dance and movement; that's why I'm a fan of Muhammad Ali. He's my favorite dancer. I think that most black fighters care more about looking good in the ring than actually winning a fight. Black people always dance whatever they do. I'm not a bleeding-heart liberal or a slummer. I like the esthetic of black people. Also, I think they are the most vital energy in American culture.

"Nowadays, my paintings as an illustrator tell anecdotes. I try to translate various assignments in the most sophisticated manner possible. But my stuff is sometimes too subtle, that obsession with style and good taste may hurt my career someday. For the time being, call me the 'Ernst Lubitsch' of illustration, and I'll be happy."

INGEBORG DAY

The Office Uniform with a System

Ingeborg Day is a thirty-four-year-old office worker in midtown Manhattan, mother of a twelve-year-old girl. She has devised a money-saving program called "Cost Per Wear" which she tells about here.

"In the winter I wear black. Two pairs of black pants, a black shirt, a black wool turtleneck, a fisherman's sweater, and a short-sleeved black sweater. I have a pair of black evening sandals and Italian boots.

"With all this black, the thing that I buy most often is tights. I never do comparison shopping for them, I just use the store that's closest to the office. I'm not going to stop wearing them if the price goes up, just like I'm not going to stop buying milk at the corner store. I get tights in special colors because it's the only color that shows in my clothes.

"In the summer I wear a pair of loose cotton pants in a purplish beige and a similar pair in blue, both two years old. This summer I bought some black drawstring pants. And last summer I went on a binge and bought three identical pairs of lined white slacks, two white t-shirts, and two white halters. They're all washable. In the summer I don't buy things that have to be

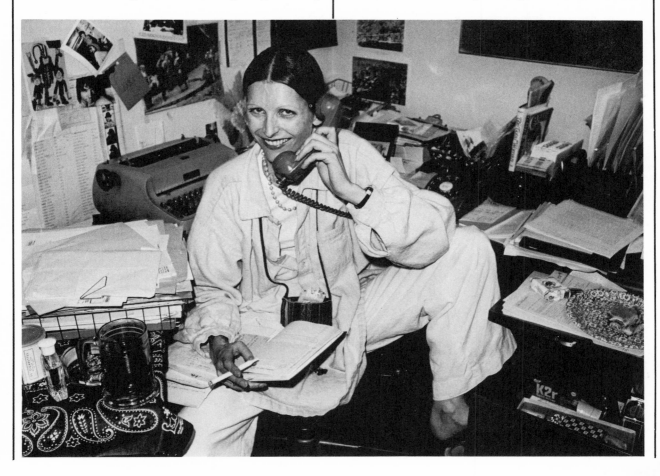

Plain pants subtly compliment an elegant dressing gown.

dry-cleaned. If you wear white and have three of each thing you can manage, even riding the subway and bus every day. I bought a white hat and a white skirt, and I wear white espadrilles. White is more practical than yellow, brown or even black, because you can use nurse's white shoe polish on the canvas—with any other color, there's nothing you can do if you spill something on them or someone steps on your foot.

"Summer and winter I wear a St. Laurent crepe de Chine skirt with narrow stitched-down pleats. I've had it since 1974, so I've worn it almost four years. It was on sale for $60, but the "Cost Per Wear" is small.

$$\frac{Price}{Number\ of\ times\ worn} = C.P.W.$$

$$\frac{\$60.00}{400} = 15¢\ per\ wearing$$

I've worn it at least 100 times a year over four years, so the CPW comes to 15¢ a wearing. In contrast, take what sounds like a cheap evening dress I bought on sale for $16 some years ago—I only wore it twice, so the CPW was $8. Compared with the 15¢ for my expensive skirt, that evening dress turned out to be a waste of money. Of course, people complain about my wearing black all the time—they say 'Has this become attached to your body?' or 'Didn't you sleep at home last night?'

"I don't dress up. No . . . that's not true, I do have three dress-up items: a Thea Porter dress, a Man Ray lip print a friend bought for me on sale for $30 that I've had since 1970, and a long black wool dress with a plain neck and no back which I bought because the designer and I both have the same first name. Recently my best friend gave me a long red velour wrap robe/dress from Betsey Johnson's.

"I always wear a simple ring given to me by my daughter, my mother's wedding ring, and a gold necklace with a guardian angel charm from my grandmother. It's all sentimental. In the summer I alternate two strands of pearls with the white T-shirts. I wear them so you can see them on the side and tuck them under the front. And recently a close friend gave me a scarab. 'It's like a pedigreed dog,' she said. 'It comes with a piece of paper, certifying that it's 3,500 years old, from such and such a dynasty.' It's now my favorite piece of jewelry.

"There are really only six areas of life you have to dress for. I've managed to get it down to three. The six areas are: bed, work, play casual, play elegant, sports, and social obligations. I've combined social obligations with play elegant. Sports, work and play casual have become the second category. Bed remains the third. If you also consider the time of year you can wear things, the clothes that fall into more than one season will give you the best CPW.

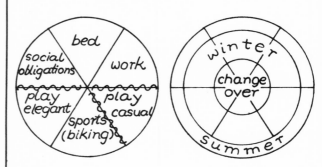

"On the east coast, winter would be the largest circle, but in other places, summer might be bigger. The French butcher's smock I just bought is going to have a low CPW because I can wear it in the summer with pants and espadrilles and in the winter with a turtleneck and boots, and all the times in between. I love it."

Uniform chic—the black T-shirt and pants with classic pearls and a Guatemalan bag.

FRAN LEBOWITZ

Grouchy Simplicity

Fran Lebowitz, author of Metropolitan Life, *is a writer of great wit and imagination, but when it comes to her own clothes she follows a strict line of quality and austerity. She owns very few clothes, yet always appears in well-tailored, neat outfits. Fran insists on following her basic ideas in getting dressed, for fear of wasting her energy on frivolity.*

"I have no colors in my clothes. The most colorful I get is with two pale-pink shirts. I get too hot if there is red around me. I'm so particular about what I wear that my parents have been afraid to buy me clothes since I was six years old. I'm so conservative I still wear clothes from high school, but I haven't worn a dress in five years. It comes down to the idea that I don't like my clothes to make me stand out. To me, if anyone gets remarked on because of what they wear, they are badly dressed.

"I can't believe what some people wear. A great majority of kids in their late teens are the worst dressed . . . incredible platform shoes, glitter, hideous fabrics . . . useless extravagance.

"The only thing I ever regretted buying was this pair of black patent-leather shoes for $65 at Charles Jourdan. They're ridiculous, but I'll wear them until they fall apart. My most precious possession is a terrific riding jacket that was made a century ago for the aunt of a friend. She was eighty when she died, wearing it, and it is still holding up impeccably. The silk lining by itself is a beauty. I wear it with $2 white cotton sailor pants.

"A fan sent me a T-shirt inscribed with all sorts of ugly lines. I hate gimmicks and it prompted me to write a few paragraphs in Interview* magazine."

* ©Fran Lebowitz

Clothes with pictures and/or writing on them—yes, another complaint. Now I'm not just talking about Vuitton bags. Or Gucci wallets. Or Hermes scarves. Designers and/or business concerns who splash their names and initials all over overpriced accoutrements of dubious quality are of course exceedingly distasteful, but I am not talking about the larger issues. Open-necked deco-ish shirts with repeating patterns of middle-sized silhouettes of sailboats. Blue jeans depicting the death of Marilyn Monroe in waterproof pastels. Dresses upon which one (but preferably two) can play Monopoly. Overalls which remind toddlers, through the use of small pink animals spouting comic strip balloons, to brush their teeth. T-shirts which proclaim the illegal sexual preferences of the wearer. Ectetera. Ectetera.

"While clothes with pictures and/or writing on them are not entirely an invention of the modern age, they are an unpleasant indication of the general state of things, which encourages people to express themselves through their clothing . . . I mean, be realistic. If people don't want to listen to you, what makes you think they want to hear from your sweater?

"There are two main reasons why we wear clothes. First, to hide figure flaws, of which the average person has at least seventeen. And second, to look cute, which is at least cheering. If some people think that nice, muted, solid colors are a bit dull, they can add some punch with stripes, plaids, checks, or if it's summer and they're girls, small dots. For those of you who feel that this is too restrictive, answer me this: If God meant for people to walk around in coats that have pictures of butterscotch sundaes on them, then why does He wear tattersal shirts?"

ANTIQUES

SHOPPING THE THRIFT STORES

Up until a few years ago, wearing some stranger's old clothes was something only the poorest people did when forced to. Can you imagine your mother buying used clothes, except in an almost-new shop with prices to match? But as everyone is discovering, it feels good to wear expensive clothes, especially when someone else paid for them the first time out. And today, it can be a positive joy to track down that one beautiful item of used clothing you have your heart set on. As chic antique clothing boutiques proliferate, even smart department stores are carrying antiques . . . and the quality never seems to run out!

Old clothes give you a sense of continuity with the past—an elegant way of life lived in luxurious fabrics of strict tailoring, a life of fluttering afternoon rituals and evening formalities. Solid old clothes give you a feeling that in this throwaway world

Tiny strips of cotton are folded, appliqued and made into this unusual jacket by Florida Indians.

there are still some things around that can last ten, twenty, thirty, forty years, or more, and remain beautiful. And if you have the instincts of a bloodhound, they can be in your very own closet!

BEING CHOOSEY

There are a few things to keep in mind when shopping for old clothes. When you come upon something that appeals to you, ask yourself if the design is timeless. Will you be able to wear a thirties dress in a comfortable, contemporary style, or will it resist all your attempts to take away its strong costume look? Unless you prefer to wear costumes instead of clothes, you will not be happy with it. A costume takes a lot of energy to wear. It's usually going to wear you; perhaps wear you out (and that's not what you're after).

Secondly, is this discovery of yours in first-rate condition? Will the fabric hold up? Will the beading stay on? Will it come back in one piece from your friendly neighbor-hood dry cleaner? And has it been cleaned often enough in its past life? Or does someone else's smell waft from the armpit of that glamorous but seldom-cleaned beauty? If it does, think twice. Perspiration may be chemically locked into the fabric, and each time you start to perspire in it, it will add its own unnerving scent—which won't be Chanel No. 5!

Third, if a piece of used clothing doesn't fit perfectly, is it close enough to your size to be fixed by a tailor or seamstress? Try it on. When thrift shopping, wear a leotard, tights, and a wraparound or button-front skirt. This way you can slip things on even if there's no dressing room. And if you like to wear high heels or boots, bring them along to get a sense of proportion when you try on dresses or pants. (Be careful with pants, because they often stretch to fit the ample aspects of just one person's derrière and can't be reshaped.)

Once you start collecting old clothes, line up a seamstress or tailor to help match up those brilliant discoveries of yours with the realities of your body. Because it seems that body shapes, as well as fashions, go in and

| **Jezebel is a top banana in New York's used clothing scene, specializing in droopy dresses and stiff Victoriana.**

out of style every few years. (Witness Marilyn Monroe's Nike-missile breasts versus Twiggy's flat chest. Yet you want to wear both fifties and sixties things, right?) Make a pact with yourself to put aside the money to *make it fit*. Fit can make the least expensive find look very elegant.

You need a sensitive, able seamstress to make an old dress look as tasty as it did back in the forties.

TYPES OF SHOPS

There are several kinds of stores that sell used clothing. In a descending level of price (though not necessarily quality), there are the antique clothing boutiques carrying exquisite hand-finished antique dresses and couture clothes; the almost-new shops that hold clothes on consignment; private-enterprise boutiques, flea-market stalls, and thrift shops that pick over other thrift shop racks and sell you their finds for a markup. The privately owned youth-oriented thrift shops are where most of the action is, since they're a trendy compromise between department store and junk shop. They're popular because we don't all have the time and guts it takes to comb through hundreds of musty old thrift shops. These shops take the worry out of being cheap.

Los Angeles is a used-clothing haven. For some reason, perhaps the high glamour quotient of living near Hollywood and a tendency to treasure things that remind one of past dreams, southern California has the most accessible, appealing, best-quality clothes around. There are stores like Anne's-Tiques in Santa Monica that sell prim hand-starched and hand-ironed Victorian-era wedding dresses in absolutely pristine condition at a quarter of their price in New York. There are hundreds of thrift shops hidden amidst the waving palms, both charitable and not, classy and not-so-classy, as well as a thriving private business in selected secondhand clothes. With practice you can shop these stores as fast as your favorite boutique.

Lesley, a tough-minded English girl who always wears used clothes, shops nothing classier than thrift shops when she's working in Los Angeles. She has the time and the practiced eye to come up with some beguiling clothes, and she really can't afford to buy any other way. One of her most prized possessions is a perfectly preserved red satin jacket with bias-bound buttonholes and tailored cuffs by Don Loper, a grand designer-to-the-stars of the fifties era. She found this treasure for 95¢ at the downtown

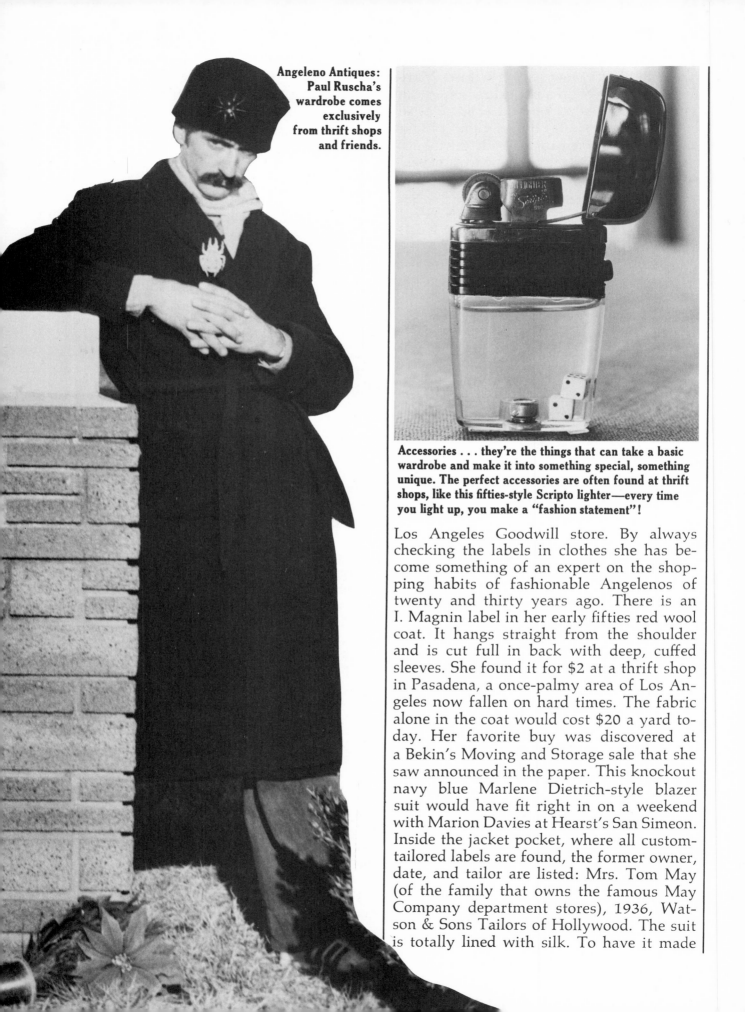

Angeleno Antiques: Paul Ruscha's wardrobe comes exclusively from thrift shops and friends.

Accessories . . . they're the things that can take a basic wardrobe and make it into something special, something unique. The perfect accessories are often found at thrift shops, like this fifties-style Scripto lighter—every time you light up, you make a "fashion statement"!

Los Angeles Goodwill store. By always checking the labels in clothes she has become something of an expert on the shopping habits of fashionable Angelenos of twenty and thirty years ago. There is an I. Magnin label in her early fifties red wool coat. It hangs straight from the shoulder and is cut full in back with deep, cuffed sleeves. She found it for $2 at a thrift shop in Pasadena, a once-palmy area of Los Angeles now fallen on hard times. The fabric alone in the coat would cost $20 a yard today. Her favorite buy was discovered at a Bekin's Moving and Storage sale that she saw announced in the paper. This knockout navy blue Marlene Dietrich-style blazer suit would have fit right in on a weekend with Marion Davies at Hearst's San Simeon. Inside the jacket pocket, where all custom-tailored labels are found, the former owner, date, and tailor are listed: Mrs. Tom May (of the family that owns the famous May Company department stores), 1936, Watson & Sons Tailors of Hollywood. The suit is totally lined with silk. To have it made today, at Bernard Weatherill Tailors in New York, would cost $400. It cost Lesley something like $3.

Lesley never fiddles with her clothes. "I never buy anything unless it fits. I like to keep the original length and proportion. I could never afford the quality I like in new clothes—that's why I buy old clothes. But I do spend a lot of time looking. It's the chase I love, the great discovery you feel when you're really struck by something!"

Artist/calligrapher Paul Ruscha is a neighbor of Lesley's who wears thrift-shop clothes as well as bits and pieces he trades around with friends or gets in exchange for his work. Artists who haunt thrift shops are always trying to one-up each other, and it leads to some very entertaining clothes! Paul's closet is hung on pipes, thrift-shop style, at one end of his studio. His prize is a monkey-fur coat given to him by an actress who got religion: she got a calligraphed Ten Commandments, and he got the coat. At night, Paul loves to go dancing in outfits like his white Tropicana Hotel pants with a blue silk, Isle of Capri, flare-collared, fifties shirt. Paul says you can always find Dior, Cardin, and St. Laurent shirts at the social aid societies ("like the Assistance League Thrift Shop on Fountain across from the Gas War"). Rich women have a quota of clothes they have to turn in to remain chummy with their friends at the league, so they bring in their hapless husband's almost-new shirts and go charge him newer ones. Paul figured all the young wives were doing this when he lived in Oklahoma City.

EXPERTISE

One of the reasons Susan Doukas moved to Los Angeles from New York was because of all the great thrift shops. Her taste leans toward unique, funny dresses with a lot of style, like her "Lauren Bacall" dress with gold studding on rust crepe and lots of sophisticated cutting. She's a definite believer in recycling, and says even when she gets rich she'll still go to thrift shops. "You can do really well if you have a little taste and not much money, especially if you look for beautiful things with a sense of humor. Certain clothes were really very silly, like the dresses of the thirties with all the intricate cutting and flaps and brooches. Dresses made statements of humor, and you could choose something you responded to because it was unique. Now fashion is just androgynous. Mass manufactured clothes have no individuality. Here are some of my pointers for shopping for used clothes:

1. Look for messy shops. A good one will have things like pants mixed up in the blouse bin. The very best bargains are in stores where you get really dirty, like the Volunteers of America in downtown L. A.

2. If you have a whole day and don't mind driving, hit the outlying areas, especially the old-guard suburbs, like Locust Valley out on Long Island.

3. Try to get an immediate sense of price. You can tell right off with shoes, first, then hats, picture frames, kitchenware. A glass for a nickel is cheap. Even though the stuff

Trucia Kushner found this beautiful Sulka silk man's robe at a used clothing store in New York City.

83

may seem depressing one day, remember shops really vary because they constantly get new shipments.

4. You must wash things to kill the bugs, and that bothers some people! If there's a smell or stain, I just scrub and scrub and send it to the cleaners. But remember, for $8 you can get the most absolutely gorgeous thirties or forties crepe dress. And if you take it in, you can make a drawstring purse from the leftover fabric.

5. If salesladies want to help you and follow you around, avoid the shop. It's not worth it. I prefer a place where I can barter. Say I find a $1.50 sweater with a couple of buttons missing or a hole in it. Usually it's okay to say, 'Can I have it for a dollar?,' especially if it's a Christian organization. In the Jewish ones they don't usually let you bargain—they just say, 'No, honey, the price is marked.' "

When a group of friends all thrift shop, they can help each other develop collections. Susan, for instance, has a closet full of bowling-league shirts and soft-drink-delivery-man's uniforms.

Susan insists her style is silly rather than chic, but she always pulls off an individual look with special moxie.

Valentina has to put together a wardrobe on the small salary she makes as production assistant and receptionist on the Cher Show. She tries her best in the midst of all that Bob Mackie-designed Cher glamour to pull off a special look. She likes to mix the old with the new, and for her the private-enterprise used-clothing store is the best bet. In the funky Silverlake section of Los Angeles where she lives is a typical shop called Aardvark's Odd Ark. Used clothing chosen with an eye for the younger customer is arranged on racks by category: used jeans, plaid shirts, overalls, Levi jackets, forties and fifties tailored jackets, suits, beaded thirties dresses, bias-cut nightgowns, Mexican felt jackets, and a multitude of sins. The most outstanding and high-priced items are displayed on the walls above the racks, rather dusty, but often the only decor in this type of low-overhead operation. And where do the clothes come from? Shops ranging from Aardvarks's on up to the used chic of Yesterday's News near Beverly Hills buy their goods from out-of-the-way thrift shops or from the sinister-sounding "rag houses" in downtown Los Angeles. Ropa Usada is one of these rag house warehouses. Room-sized bundles of clothing from the Midwest are piled to the ceiling and sold in one-thousand-pound lots without being cleaned. A thousand pounds of clothes can run $200 to $500. The bundles then have to be sorted by the buyer and the best things winnowed out and cleaned. Some of the smaller dealers complain that the used-clothing business is getting so profitable it's being run like the Mafia, that Beverly Hills-style boutiques have a complete monopoly on the rag house bundles.

People in the West and down South hold outdoor swap meets year-round, while others have to wait for the summer months. One of the Angelenos' favorite gathering spots is the Hollywood Swap Meet, located in an empty corner parking lot on Santa Monica Boulevard in West Hollywood. It's a lively area filled with picnic tables, makeshift dressing rooms, and jerrybuilt clothes racks. Just plain folks as well as Zsa Zsa Gabor, Ruth Buzzi, Lena Horne, Shelley Winters, Sonny Bono, Carol Lynley, and

Valentina eyes the reindeer rack at her local L.A. store.

Cher drop by to try stuff on. The sellers rent space to display their wares and the lot is open every day of the week. We found an apricot, hand-sewn crepe de Chine bed jacket for $2; beautiful pure silk nightgowns with hand-stitching and hand-made lace appliqués (perfect for transferring to a T-shirt or dress if the rest of the fabric is frayed) for $3 to $10; hundreds of pairs of used jeans arranged by size for $4 or $5; Air Force flight suits for $25–$35; sailor tops, military uniforms, and safari jackets, and typically Californian standbys like kimonos, Mexican felt jackets, Oriental-theme satin baseball jackets, and Hawaiian print shirts. (The best-priced and most amiable stall is run by Ruthie, but she's only there on Fridays.) Another popular swap meet is the massive gathering held on weekends in the Hollywood Bowl. It's so big it can make you dizzy.

San Francisco is a tremendous place to find stylish used clothing because of the flashy transvestite and gay scene crystallized by the Cockettes in the early seventies. Stores that cater to this taste, like Casey's Faded World and the Flying A, have higher prices but very select merchandise. It's nice to have a gay friend—he can often steer you in the direction of the most chic, and the most cheap, shop in your town.

It's always smart to get shopping advice from people who make money from their clothes. Carrie White, who runs a beauty salon in Beverly Hills, rented out some things from her personal wardrobe for the film *Shampoo*, set in 1968. ("1968, can you believe it! They're already being collected!")

Carrie says to stake out five thrift shops rather than spreading yourself thin over fifteen. Whenever you travel, check the most remote places for shops (like Cathedral City, which is ten minutes out of Palm Springs), or at least go one block off the main drag. She looks first for colors and patterns that will ease her eyes when she sees herself in the salon mirror at work. She always checks the thrift-shop drawers, which a lot of people forget, and finds doilies, ribbons, scarves, bathing suits; napkins which make great skirts and pieces for lengthening jeans; and white lace to lengthen white pants. And since Carrie has four kids, she's always looking for children's hand-crafted clothes. Carrie loves the sport and the fun of it. "In nine years, no customer has ever seen me in the same thing twice!"

Another person who makes money by

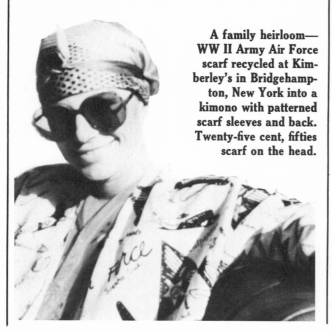

A family heirloom—WW II Army Air Force scarf recycled at Kimberley's in Bridgehampton, New York into a kimono with patterned scarf sleeves and back. Twenty-five cent, fifties scarf on the head.

The ultimate luck is to dig up a twenties extravaganza in a musty, old thrift shop. When luck strikes, spend.

collecting old clothes is Steve Starr. The Steve Starr Studio in Chicago is home for a truly spectacular collection of period clothing, some for sale. Steve says he collects "art deco, art moderne, art ultra, and twentieth-century costumes and accessories." Every year he stages the Steve Starr Vanity, which stars his clothes, decade by decade, worn by an all-singing, all-dancing, cast of clothes freaks and models parading through a series of elaborate production numbers and film clips. It may well be the most entertaining event of the year in Chicago, a home-grown *That's Entertainment*. Since he has so many first-quality dresses and accessories, he is often reluctant to sell his favorites, which he keeps for the Vanity and

Wendy Whitelaw in a favorite brown crepe antique dress with inset velvet bows, teeny-tiny buttons, and a beige silk sash tied at the waist.

uses in producing and styling photographs, many for *Playboy*. He's now working on a full-color collection of these photos, which should be a tremendous source book for period clothes.

In London, the painter Duggie Fields and about twenty or thirty friends put on their own "jumble sales" by hiring a church hall and bringing things to sell. "The rental goes to the church charities, and what we make we keep for ourselves. We advertise the sale in the local papers, list it in *Time Out* magazine, and design posters to put in neighborhood shops. Hundreds of people come. It's fun, and it's a good way to get rid of your old stuff and get new from your friends. It's good recycling, and at the same time you can make $100 in an afternoon just for cleaning out your closet.

"The clothes are all piled up—our first jumble sale was chaos—and as soon as the doors open, people run in, grabbing. It's like being in a chicken coop. But it's a nice afternoon, and it's fun to see who turns up. I even see people stealing. They know I know they haven't paid, but I'm not going to say a thing . . . things gotta go!

"I only buy clothes in stores if I need something I can't find here. They're not necessarily fashionable stores. My favorite is called 'Sex' in the World's End . . . bits of furs, porno embroidered T-shirts, and humorous clothes. My idea of wearing clothes is to make myself smile. I like that in others too. I don't think clothes should be serious."

In New York, the used clothing prices

Duggie Fields' sensibility is born of jumble sale chaos.

are much higher than they are in Europe or on the Coast. Some of our favorite stores in New York are Everybody's Thrift Shop, Jezebel (on the West Side), Cherchez!, and especially Harriet Love's in the SoHo district south of the Village. Harriet's been selling antique clothing for years, and now her specials run from beautifully embroidered turn-of-the-century white petticoats, slips, and camisoles to Annie Hall-style men's pleated pants for women.

One of the best places to find rich New Yorker's castoffs is where they vacation, like the Palm Beach Thrift Shop in Florida. Beautifully tailored three-piece suits can be found here for $10, and with tailoring, a suit for the office can cost only $35. One New York businessman has three $10 English-tailored suits he bought at the Palm Beach Thrift Shop: two formerly lived in New York, one in Chicago. Along with a navy cashmere coat from Saks, also used, they make up his entire office wardrobe, and no one is any the wiser.

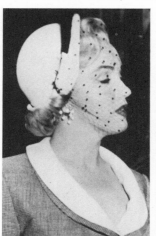

Blondes do have more fun, especially when they're hiding behind an old-fashioned mysterious bit of veiling.

Garbo put this outfit together forty years ago, but by smart antiques shopping, you can put it together today.

ANTIQUES

For some fashionable women, the ultimate chic is dressing in couturier clothes of the past. An eccentric editor at Italian *Vogue* dresses entirely in antique Poiret couturier originals that are terribly elegant yet contemporary in feeling. Who could make a more glorious dress than Schiaparelli, or a more elegant suit than Chanel? If you set your sights on originals like these, you have to be extremely lucky (of course, the first step to "luck" is to learn as much as you can about the couture), and it helps to cultivate rich relatives or friends, unless you are prepared to spend your life's savings!

Most of the truly classic couture clothes are now being donated by estates to museum collections for the inevitable tax write-offs. Thousands of beautiful things are locked away in the climate-controlled storage rooms of the Chicago Historical Society, the Metropolitan Museum, and the Museum of the City of New York. Entire wardrobes, right down to the needle-toed, stiletto-heeled Charles Jourdan black faille pumps, arrive by chauffeured limousines and are carried into these grand museums, never to be worn again except by plaster mannequins. Some designer clothes are still at large, though they are increasingly rare. The owner of an antique clothing shop in New York has two St. Laurent couture dresses, because, she says, "they are a lot nicer than the things that are being made now. I bought them for a good price and can resell them at a reasonable profit. I've been collecting clothes for about ten years, going to places like Canada and south to Georgia, but now it's costing too much to go out and look." She has sold a Chanel, a St. Laurent, and a Fortuny dress. If you don't have hundreds in disposable income, your best bet is to try Canada and Georgia yourself!

GREAT FINDS

When shopping for used clothing, whether you are in a pricey on-consignment store or a dirty old thrift shop, be sure to keep your eyes peeled for the following:

Luscious fabrics, like pure **silk,** in nightgowns, slips, loose undershorts, chemises, bed jackets. All sorts of scarves, especially the $1 bias-cut, long, thirties silks (now selling at around $30 in antique clothing shops). Well-cut silk shirts. Lovely silk

Expert thrift-shoppers keep their eyes peeled for pure silks like this arty-looking, loose-cut blouson.

neckties, silk squares, and neck scarves.

Cotton petticoats, lace shirts, Victorian dresses with tight bodices, men's and women's shirts, straight nightgowns, cowboy shirts, cotton flannel plaid shirts, pedal-pushers, slacks, and safari outfits.

Pure **wool** is found in women's tailored suits, coats of gabardine, melton, cashmere, tweed, and challis, tight or big mid-calf skirts, and sweaters. If you're looking for a sweater, be sure to look through the children's bin, because the French size their sweaters 1, 2, and 3, and the ladies who work in volunteer thrift shops aren't going to know this, but you are. In fact, it helps to familiarize yourself with European sizing.

The French sizes 1–2–3– for T-shirts run a bit tighter than American S–M–L, because the French prefer shirts to be a bit more clinging. English dress sizes usually run one size smaller than American. A size 10, for instance, would be the equivalent of our 8. And continental sizing for dresses, blouses, pants, sweaters, and so on runs 38–40–42–44, roughly the equivalent of 6–8–10–12. For slips and bras, 80–85–90–95 is 32–34–36–38. European shoes don't have the range of widths ours do, and the sizes 36–37–38–39–40 are roughly 5 – 6 – 7 – 8 – 9 . Of course, as with anything you find at a thrift shop, try it on.

Men can look for beautiful wool overcoats, tailored suits, sport jackets, formal evening wear, fifties Eisenhower jackets, letter jackets, and pleated slacks. A tailor can make you feel like a million bucks for an investment of $25 and a morning spent digging through likely looking shops. A

True costumes like this demand a self-confident stance and a bit of discipline, qualities exuded by the two sisters, above. Such old clothes were once cared for by a battery of seamstresses, laundresses, dressmakers and ladies' maids. Delicate antique clothes still demand very special hand care and a slower, self-contained manner of moving. Start dancing, and precious old fabrics rip and shred and seams reach the breaking point.

A fifties jewel-encrusted, beaded cardigan with matching knit skirt—both from Macy's antiques corner—flashed up with Woolworth's bangles and skyscraper sandals!

slim woman can look beautiful in a man's suit if she has it tailored to fit perfectly and wears it with the humor of Bianca Jagger: walking stick, hat and veil, a crisp cotton shirt or a bright silk blouse unbuttoned practically to the waist, with a tiny gold chain underneath.

Another material to look for is beautifully worn **leather,** which can always be relined; tent-shaped trenchcoats for men or women, suede jackets and sport jackets, brown or black motorcycle jackets with a diagonal zipper. Some people have good luck with shoes, like worn brown English oxfords, expensive old high heels, and weatherbeaten riding boots.

And for extraspecial evenings: fur boas, pleated or gathered taffeta skirts, soft velvet dresses or smoking jackets, all sorts of fancy cocktail dresses and ball gowns, and men's velvet evening jackets. One friend of ours found custom-made tails with a label from Barcelona for $5, including the

A terrycloth bathrobe wrapped with a long knitted scarf becomes a spring coat for boutique-owner Dianne Schools.

starched front. His tailor fit it to him for $30, and the couple of times he's worn it to formal parties he's had great fun imagining the stiff and rather large Spaniard who inhabited the tails before he did.

So, if you want to be cheap and stay terribly chic, remember that your best allies are thrift shops, used-clothing stores, antique clothing boutiques, swap meets in empty lots or out-of-town drive-ins, European flea markets (like Portobello Road in London, the Thieves Market in Amsterdam, or the Marche aux Puces in Paris), street fairs, block parties, and individual garage sales. If you're still unfulfilled, have your own "jumble sale."

A little-known bit of forties chic: The "captain's dinner jacket" in a light wool gabardine, from the collection of Chicago's Steve Starr Studio, worn by Mr. Starr himself.

If you have to go white tie, try the thrift shop route. A fifties spaghetti-strap gown is the perfect companion.

DISCOUNTS

Aside from all these used-clothing resources, smart dressers have always known that you can finish off a look very cheaply at mass-market discount and five-and-dime stores. Great bargains are there for the finding at chains like Woolworth's: smock tops;

Thrift shops are a godsend for parents on a tight budget. You can always find kids' wonderful hand-made things here.

An antique Philippine tea dress Larissa found at Harriet Love's in N.Y. Without an underslip, it's a party dress.

printed, pleated, or visored scarves; arm-loads of beads, pearls, and plastic bracelets; hooded sweatshirts and pants; bikinis or $1 Rio-style pants; short shorts; plain and souvenir T-shirts in cotton and terrycloth; country bandanas; summer shifts; and lots of interesting shoes, like the plastic, fisherman's Mary Jane, a ballet slipper flat you can wear on the street, the Japanese rubber-and-straw-soled shoe with a velvet thong, and the canvas cross-strapped old ladies' shoe. The drawback these days with the discount chains is that they are trying to merchandise "looks," which means that the quality of the fabric and construction is going down while you pay more for a "fashion" that will probably bore you next

Sofi Bollack and little Eleonore created the lush look of Victorian teatime with the help of a friendly thrift shop and plump pillows made of fancy remnants.

The formal social dance of the past has been bypassed by the hustle of today. But by outfitting ourselves in luxurious antique clothing, we can afford to partake in the old rituals. Here, Pierre Clementi in Steppenwolf approximates fin de siecle seriousness.

year or even next month. Too bad, but you can still snoop around and find classic designs if you persist.

Big-volume department stores, like Alexander's, Ohrbach's and Macy's, often carry the newest ready-to-wear looks from Europe at very low prices, but you have to shop carefully and know just what you're looking for so you don't get swamped by all the merchandise.

Ethnic shopping areas will often yield great buys. In New York, Jewish merchants sell their wares in crowded stalls on Orchard Street, and a lot of almost-wholesale buys from Seventh Avenue manufacturers are mixed in with the cheap merchandise. Also on the Lower East Side are the Russian shops around St. Mark's Place, which carry about the same merchandise as the government-run tourist shops in the capitals of Eastern European countries—peasant blouses, challis scarves, carved wood boxes, painted eggs. On Fourteenth Street there is a vast hubbub of Puerto Ricans shopping discount stores with bins

The jacket: Chinese silk brocade. Era: pre-Communist. Point of purchase: Palm Beach Thrift Shop, $10 (plus tax).

along the sidewalk, and way uptown is La Marqueta, the enclosed Puerto Rican market area with stalls running under the elevated tracks of the New York Central Railroad. These street markets are not limited to clothing and household goods—you can always pick up some compatible food, like blinis on St. Mark's or Caribbean plantains in La Marqueta.

Some people stroll by Fifth Avenue department store windows for entertainment, but shopping older urban areas can be a much less expensive pastime. No matter what city you visit, seek out the old neighborhoods with their thrift shops and discount stores. You can spend a fine afternoon looking for wonderful bargains, and finish it off by devouring an adventurous local meal.

Genevieve Waite loves her
soft apricot crepe de Chine bed
jacket for summer parties.
Totally hand-stitched,
it was $2 at the Hollywood Swap Meet.
Her son Tamerlaine is less fond
of his new school uniform.

DONNA KARAN

Designing Woman

Donna Karan has been designing at Anne Klein since 1971 and she's now reached the venerable age of twenty-nine. She's a smart cookie with a real feel for the Anne Klein customer . . . a woman who likes to dress in fine designer sportswear. Donna ought to know the customer. At fourteen she was selling up a storm in a Long Island dress shop. Her passion for making women look better never stopped. Three years ago Donna said she thought a woman could get away with a pair of good black

Donna giggles with a model before a show.

pants, a good black skirt, black turtleneck, a pair of boots in a neutral color, straight-leg jeans, and a fabulous belt. "The big word is function," she said then. "Everything has to work together." And today? She's still all for neutral colors. How does she feel about tailored classics like the blazer when the fashion code word is soft? And what about the rules in the Dress for Success book: a woman will move on the job if she wears a sort of uniform made up of a conservative, blue three-piece skirted suit, a light or white blouse, and plain, low-heeled pumps. With an executive's briefcase, gold pen, and attitude. And never, never boots....

"The tailored blazer I did a few years ago isn't out. But fashion would be boring if it didn't change. Today there's much more inventiveness in fashion. Finding that one accent that changes how you look. Pulling clothes together you usually wouldn't pull together. Not looking as matched. Yesterday, for instance, I was wearing a pair of 'Garbo' pants that I did four years ago. I wore a different shirt—crepe de Chine, unbuttoned, with the sleeves rolled up—then tied a softer sash belt around it and wore my ballet slippers. I was working with a soft look. One day I might wear big . . . a big pair of corduroy pants and a bulky sweater and the next day, go slim. That's why I don't think there's any dictation of a proportion in fashion today. It has to do with how I feel today. Ladylike, sporty, sexy.

"I never want to go back to feeling con-

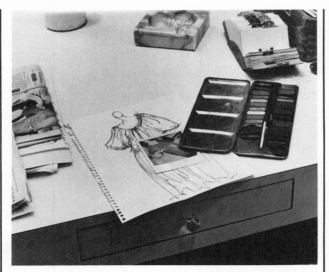

stricted in clothes, putting myself together uptight, like in an A-line skirt with no movement to it. If you can't get your hands into a pair of pockets and move around in your clothes, it's not worth it! I can wear a piece from my collection year after year, but I'll change the way I wear it, the attitude. Like the big suede skirt I did three years ago; that was the biggest investment of anything! It's not that there's a major change in fashion now, it's just how you're wearing your clothes. Like taking a sleeve, pushing it up, wearing a shirt more open, sexy.

"I was approached to write a book like Dress for Success. But I believe that a woman's professional clothes have to come from the inside out. The clothes are never going to make the woman. To be successful today a woman has to be professional, have a clean-cut head. Keep her body and mind in shape. Stay clean and kempt. And be smart enough to look in a mirror to judge for herself what's right and what's wrong on her. Clothes have nothing to do with success. But I guarantee you that if a woman's together, she's going to know enough about herself to look outta sight!

"I believe that feminism comes through a woman's body, from the inside out. A woman who is uptight is never going to get free. Her movements . . . her body should be toned up, able to move, not stiff. Then she puts on clothes that work for her, that move with her. The uptight woman is just too afraid to look in the mirror. You've got to experiment and not be afraid. The European woman, for instance, works at it. A lot. She's not afraid of change. With change you can find out about yourself and what your style is. Believe me, when a woman puts on that thing that looks right on her, she's going to feel great! And when you have an assurance about yourself, honey, you can walk into any room and command anything. But you've got to work at it. It doesn't come easily."

Above: designer's table . . . sketch, box of Biba cosmetics, Rolodex, ashtray, WWD, coffee mug.
The sketch is just one of dozens that will end up swatched with fabrics like those on the wall behind Donna.

EWA RUDLING

Ragpicker Deluxe

Ewa Rudling is a deluxe ragpicker. She directs and paints her life in muted tones. In her large white-and-silver Paris photography studio everything is mobile. Ewa uses all of her furniture and her own clothes as accessories in her detailed and refined photographs.

"I want to be like a mop of quality. Nobody can ever say I look dirty, because I dress on purpose in dirt tones. I dye most of my clothes dust brown, dust gray, and so on. A few years ago I saw the film Trash and was shocked to see someone furnishing their house with things retrieved from garbage and getting dressed out of rags. At that time I was really living in luxury with a wealthy husband in a three-floor house surrounded by a garden.

"When I left, it was total poverty and a long struggle. When you are, or when you become, poor, you also become very inventive. You find yourself taking in things you normally would not have looked at before. Like an ant, you gather other people's discards that, with a little thought, they could put to use themselves.

"After a while I accumulated so much stuff that I started making money from it to pay for my photography. I would hold 'chiffon parties'—I would take all the things I thought were good to sell: clothes, jewelry, objects, suitcases, shoes, hang them all over the studio, and let everyone know that a sale was going on. People would bring other people and I would get rid of all the clothes in one go, and often also acquire new ones or simply exchange. It's the best way to clean out your closet and make money.

"Of course, by that time you have left your pride far behind you . . ."

At one time, sportswomen looked precisely like sportsmen—there was no room for good looks in competition. But now we can have our cake and eat it too. Style is so free we can look as feminine in a man's football jersey as we can in a ruffled tennis dress. Today, more and more women are wearing professional athletic clothes as an almost day-in, day-out style of dressing. There are several reasons for the popularity of authentic sportswear, but their main attraction is functional, unchanging, unflappable design. Sports clothes are built for speed, endurance, power, and winning. And who can't use a little injection of that in everyday life?

With the advent of color TV, pro sports picked up electric acrylic colors—the Oakland A's suited up in Fort Knox gold, trimmed with Pacific Ocean green; and everyone acquired a taste for nice, tight-fitting, stretch uniforms over well-muscled, shapely bodies. Professional athletes say that looking good makes them play better; their uniforms give them that winning feeling.

Also, some sports clothes offer the cheap thrill of discovery. A Cheap Chic adept is going to go out and find the ones that haven't been discovered by Seventh Avenue because they offer economy with true style.

Last year a friend of ours was driving through Ireland and stopped at an out-of-the-way sporting-goods shop in Galway hoping to discover some new well-designed uniform. The soccer things looked rather promising—those great T-shirts and striped socks—until she got back to London and visited Biba's department store, where the soccer motif had been so thoroughly run through the fashion grinder that little 75¢ soccer-ball-shaped change purses were up for sale next to the cash register. She decided there was nothing left to discover on God's green earth. But then came the import of the sport of motocross, still relatively unknown outside southern California and the Northeast, where the major events take place. She discovered a whole new world of clothes—high, sturdy leather boots with bright contrasting panels in the front, and beautifully cut pants with diagonally quilted leather pads along the sides of the hip and thigh. She was ecstatic. Since she was tall and skinny, the motocross pants looked great, despite the padding.

The cheapest places to find authentic

American cheese of sportswear, bristling with unnecessary buttons, flaps, cuffs, and seams. Sports clothes still have the magic of childhood game clothes.

FLEET OF FOOT

Warm-up suits give you that fast-on-your-feet look even if you don't jog or play tennis every day. What thief would risk snatching your purse if you look like a champion sprinter? **Warm-up suits** are being manufactured in more styles and brighter colors. If you feel conservative, buy yourself a high-school-style warm-up suit in gray, fuzzy-lined sweatshirt material with a front-pocketed top. It's as comfortable for sleeping on cold nights as for shopping on crisp afternoons. The gray sweatshirts can also be dyed in darker colors to fit your mood. A $7 sweatshirt can be ordered from J. C. Penney's catalog in pale blue, yellow, red, or green, with matching $7 snug-fitting sweatpants, which won't look or feel as floppy as the loose, baggy, sixties style. Oleg Cassini makes a jersey warm-up and competition set with jacket, pants, sleeveless T-shirt, and tiny shorts, all in bright colors. The women athletes wore them for the ABC-TV Women's Superstar event at the Astrodome. Suzy Chaffee looked especially snazzy in her acid-yellow short-shorts combined with multicolored Peruvian-style patterned knee socks and black professional warm-up shoes.

Tennis whites are so popular these days that demand is rumored to be more than

athletic clothes are sometimes out of the way, but it's worth bypassing your expensive local pro shop or tennis boutique. The best way to buy professional athletic wear is to look up sporting-goods stores in the Yellow Pages and give them a call. If they don't have what you're looking for, it's almost as convenient to order things by mail. You'll have to ask a male friend for a size approximation if you're sending for boys' or men's sporting uniforms, but if they don't fit, most mail-order houses will usually exchange them. Try the big mail-order catalogs, and for the less-popular uniforms, like rugby or soccer, send for information from the manufacturers listed in the back of this book.

The good feeling you get from honest-to-goodness sports clothes comes from their purity of design. They haven't been through the fashion mill of Seventh Avenue, and they still have that legitimate feeling. They're not yet made into the processed

the manufacturers can churn out. In the suburbs, many women have taken to wearing inexpensive, easy-care tennis dresses as their everyday uniform. If you have nice legs, a tennis dress gives you a good excuse to show them off. One problem with tennis dresses these days is that they have become a fashion item, and dashing, simple design has given way to all sorts of "cute" motifs and silly details. Tennis stars like Billie Jean King and Françoise Durr wear these flashy dresses because they consider themselves, quite rightly, to be in show business. Are you?

Sneakers are basic Cheap Chic footwear. It used to be that fashion started at the top and worked its way down; the feet were just an afterthought. But here we are in an era of tight money, and we don't have that much to spend on body coverings. To save money, we can displace our fascination with the minutiae of style and status to the foot—a foot dressed in a very expensive permutation of what was once a cheap shoe, the sneaker. Sneaker demand is up almost 25 percent this year. Of course, the sneaker is not only stylish, it's Good for You, like chicken soup on a cold day. Sneakers bring you back to childhood, high spirits, and magically high leaps.

In the haute monde of sneakerdom there is a competition of status symbols which easily rivals the Fifth Avenue battles of Gucci, Hermès, and Mark Cross. Sneakers don't have designers' names, they have signs: stripes, wedges, chevrons, and stars of status. And they have endorsements by the new media stars, athletes like Billie Jean King and Walt "Clyde" Frazier.

It started with the war between Adidas and Puma, companies owned by feuding German brothers. *Sports Illustrated* did an exposé on their buy-out of the athletes at the Mexico City Olympics, and for the first time, Cheap Chic students were exposed to the full stylistic possibilities of $30 leather-and-suede athletic shoes. Wrestling shoes, boxing shoes, high-tops, training shoes, track shoes, football shoes, soccer shoes, officiating shoes, tennis shoes, handball shoes! It was a mere hop, skip, and a jump from track and basketball shoes into tennis shoes and out onto the streets. Now you can choose from the Converse star, Pony chevron, Adidas triple stripe, and the Puma flying wedge. Somehow, those $11.98 Levi's feel a lot livelier when a pair of $30 wear-forever leather sneakers is peeking out under the cuff! If you want a man's sneaker, buy them 1½ sizes smaller than women's sizes.

SPEEDSTERS

Grand Prix drivers have highly romantic images. Just think of Paul Newman, Jackie Stewart, Steve McQueen, or Mike Hailwood. Yet the actual competition uniforms for speed are terribly uncomfortable and

The precision of a chronometer when seconds count.

hot. Their function is to protect the racer from contact with the ground at speeds hovering around one hundred miles per hour; and, in the case of Formula cars, to protect the driver from fire in case of an accident. None of these uniforms really breathe, which is one reason, along with fear and excitement, why professional racers often sweat off six pounds driving a two-hour race. But if you want to look like a Grand Prix driver without all the sweat, you can find Nomex-style, one-piece, mechanics' jumpsuits like the drivers wear. Bright orange is the sexiest color. Tight is the sexiest fit. (You'll need a seamstress to get it tight, unless you're a sewing-machine genius.)

Motorcycle gear, no matter how hot or uncomfortable, is still an evocative style of dress. "Leathers" have symbolized anger,

Racy jumpsuits built with style for speed and adventure. 109

Terry Melville: a plain
gray sweatshirt and
sweatpants. She wears
them weekends, working,
even out at night . . .
watch!

Sweatshirt in the office?
Sure, over a white cotton
man's shirt, with a soft
wool riding jacket,
hankie in the pocket.
Terry turns up the collar
of her shirt and ties an
old bowtie, just so.

Far right,
Weekends? The sweat-
suit again. With a 59¢
cotton farmer's scarf
knotted around the neck.
A man's patterned silk
vest from a used-clothing
store, taken in by the
neighborhood tailor. A
plastic stuffed-olive bracelet (her favorite) with an
art-deco bangle in olive
green. The cowboy belt
comes from Uncle Wally,
who works for the rail-
road in Ohio. The three-
tiered, light cotton gauze
skirt comes from India.
The cat comes without
pedigree, and is known as
Sam. And the finishing
touch is bright red
athletic socks (99¢) with
metallic copper flats from
Shoe Biz.

Disco sweatsuit? John Travolta might not approve, but Terry does it up with a hot-purple fur boa from Macy's, fluff from New York's flower district, expensive ankle-wrapped evening sandals, and a tiny Oriental brocade evening bag. Plus a beautifully embroidered silk kimono found in an antique clothing boutique.

Snowy flirting in stylish wools from the local sports store.

you are "molding your body to the terrain in a lyrical fashion. Freestyle is basically a feminine sport, intuitive and developmental, as opposed to pure, competitive, rational, aggressive male sports."

Of course, you can wear the uniforms of these aggressive male sports without competing, and if you're interested, here are a few team sports possibilities.

meanness, speed, and rebellion ever since Marlon Brando and the Hell's Angels. Leathers are particularly effective in black if you want to look tough! And they wear forever. A classic leather motorcycle jacket can take you through many cold winters in warmth and style—and if you happen to own a motorcycle, so much the better.

If you tire of black or brown, you can have a set of bright racing leathers custommade by Bates in soft, thick leather with a zip-front jacket, contrasting zip sleeves, and black piping trim. To go full speed, get tight matching pants with a contrasting racing stripe up the side. It's hard for a motorist to miss you in Kawasaki green!

Ski clothes have always been very expensive; but behind the high prices lay good fabrics and excellent construction. Unless you live in a terribly cold climate, it is rather difficult to wear ski clothes as everyday wear except for the accessories like little knit caps and long johns. The beautifully stretchable one-piece ski outfits are like a second skin in freestyle skiing, where, according to Olympic skiier Suzy Chaffee,

TEAM SPORTS

Team uniforms can be raided to yield colorful jerseys, knickers, shorts, socks, and mini beach covers. Use your imagination—combine Rollie Finger's socks with Walt Frazier's shorts and an Yves St. Laurent silk shirt (or even jockeys' silks)!

Basketball players wear great rayon jerseys with contrasting binding on a low-scooped neck and cut-in armholes, or sleeved versions with a contrasting neck and set-in sleeves. Either style is in a supple, silky weave. Some men think a cut-in basketball jersey makes a woman look like a jock. But that's their problem! Swimwear designers have picked up on basketball trunks and copied them for men's trunks. The originals are synthetic satin boxer shorts with wide, stretch waistbands and stripes around the bottom or up the sides. Why buy a French designer's "tap pants" when you can get basketball shorts that have twice as much sass?

Basketball socks have contrasting stripes mid-calf, and some are built to have a "self-stirrup," which means they look like a pair of baseball-style socks: the foot and heel are cut out over a pair of contrasting, full-foot socks.

Hockey has a violent aura. If you're feeling particularly mean someday, you might want to suit up in a hockey jersey with a classic lace-up neck, inset saddle shoulders, and long sleeves with a white stripe inset above the elbow. A rayon-cotton fabric

The quick feet of Pele, the most famous soccer player in the world, move with the speed of the Puma he wears.

gives the jersey a good combination of silkiness and absorption, and they're very effective as minidresses. Heavy cotton socks reach mid-thigh, with stirrups under the feet and wide stripes above the ankle. The pants themselves are unwearable. They're just a visual cover-up for side, tail, thigh, and crotch guards, an assemblage of pad pockets. But those socks are wonderful.

Football pants with the laced fly and web belts are nice in white duck, but like hockey pants they tend to be designed more for protective pads than for the body. Football jerseys are an American classic with their double shoulders and yokes, striped arms,

The padded shirt softens the blows of rugby.

and gusseted armpits, and they are long and loose enough for summer dresses. Small sizes from the boys' department are nice for layering. One of the new fabrics they come in is a nylon mesh knit.

The psychological importance of color in competitive clothes is seen in the old home-team rule—a high-school team playing on their home turf was allowed to wear white uniforms. They felt white made them appear gigantic to their opponents and gave them the winning edge.

Soccer is becoming more and more popular in the States. Although it's equally as bone crushing as football or hockey, soccer jerseys have lace-up necks, short or long sleeves with contrasting collars and stripes, short shorts, and brightly striped socks with turnover cuffs which pull over the knee on women. Rugby jerseys in cotton with drill collars and button-placket front openings are very sporty in solids or stripes. Goalie pants for soccer players come with padded hips. (If you want to look even more curvaceous in shorts, check out Frederick's of Hollywood's padded girdles!)

Baseball uniforms are made of several layers. The raglan-sleeved, braid-trimmed, cotton flannel top snaps over a baseball undershirt which has solid-color sleeves and a white body. The knicker-length pants are worn over high-cut, striped stirrup hose and contrasting inner socks. You should check out the layered socks. Add a snappy high-crowned baseball cap and everyone will get hungry for hot dogs, mustard and Beer Day at Wrigley Field.

Letter jackets are a traditional "civilian" counterpart to all this competitive regalia. Like *American Graffitti*, they epitomize the hot-rod era of the fifties and sixties. Sporting-goods supply stores that carry uniforms

Skateboarding is great for the body!

Get healthier and happier jogging your way around the city or country as Sue Murray and Ingrid Boulting do.

Japanese designer Issey Miyake likes to "shock people with ideas." Study these clothes and you will find motocross-style knee pads on the leather pants, flat English riding boots and football-jersey-sized tops over tights. All rather stunning ideas .

Waiting for the right moment—leather clad, ready to go.

often carry letter jackets. They have been the rage in Paris for sometime now and sell for $100 over there. The classic letter jacket comes with leather sleeves and slash-pocket trim; a reprocessed wool body; stretchy striped collar, cuffs, and waist, and a snap front. If you don't want to spring for a jacket, a letter sweater is always stylish around the Beach Boys and the Dell Vikings. And a cheerleader's heavy sweater with crew neck is the cat's meow.

INDIVIDUAL SPORTS

Fencing jackets are usually too stiff to wear comfortably, but they have a unique, time-worn cut and come in pleasant cotton fabrics.

Judo is a more promising area for Cheap Chic: a judo ghi is made of pure cotton duck with a wrap front and dropped shoulders. We have seen them made in a diamond-quilted cotton duck with triple stitching on the sleeves. They look beautiful over soft white pants, but be careful about picking the color of the belt you wear! You don't want to get challenged on what you thought was merely a point of fashion.

Golf is the sport responsible for introducing those bright, bold colors into weekend sports clothes. Professional golfers like Carol Mann always look terrific in their bright mini golf skirts and matching tops, socks, and gloves. But that's because they have contracts with the manufacturers and can afford all the mix and match, since the clothes are free. Golf clothes are really rather difficult to put together with others, because the trim of the skirt is usually quite strong and demands a matching top. If you can't afford several sets of golf clothes, perhaps the best item from the golfer's repertoire is the visor, which looks especially striking over a crisp cotton scarf tied peasant-style at the back of the head. Golfers' fingerless gloves are rather interesting, and the classic fringed golfing shoes look beautiful (without the cleats) for city or country walks, sort of like saddle shoes with an extra spin on them.

If your self-image tends toward **hiking** into the sunset with a copy of *Field And Stream*, the L. L. Bean catalog from Freeport, Maine, is a must. They have everything from the puff-ball eiderdown ski jackets you see on every school kid to all the woodland fantasies: an Australian bush hat with built-in mosquito netting, Lees Frisco corduroy jeans, wading shoes, fishing jackets, hiking boots, rain suits, suede musette bags, leather and twill haversacks, and a virtual wonderland of roughing-it paraphernalia which translates perfectly to city living.

The personal twist that makes active sports clothes amusing to wear every day lies in taking them out of the context of their particular sport and customizing them to your whims. Mix a baseball shirt with a wide seersucker skirt and wrap it with a soft leather belt. Wear an oatmeal wool tunic over bright hockey socks and a turtleneck in the winter. Wear satin boxer shorts with nothing else. And put a tough but well-fitting leather motorcycle jacket over a skimpy silk Halston dress. Use these clothes with a certain disdain for their original function but an appreciation for their functional style, and they will inspire you to keep a lean, lithe, lanky body and an aura of nonchalant sexuality.

HELENE DE BARCZA

College Clothes on $150 a Year

A college student on a tight budget, Helene has nevertheless managed to work up her own personal style. She's nineteen and a freshman at Hunter College in New York.

"There aren't as many jeans and boots around school as there used to be. I think people want to look nicer. So you see more espadrilles and longer skirts, dresses made of that Indian muslin with big belts around the waist.

"Since I only have a budget of about $150 for the school year, I have to be really careful with everything I buy. Most of my clothes are in solids; I have only a few stripes and prints. I wear a lot of boys' shirts, Eagle Brothers shirts from my old school uniform. I have six- and seven-year-old hand-me-down turtlenecks, a couple of sweaters that are two or three years old, lots of jeans from the army-surplus store and a longish dress I found at a department store for $20. But I always wear scarves, which makes things look special. A lot of my money went for my boots—the leather ones cost $60 and the denim ones were $30 at Chandler's. Then

I've got some leather espadrilles and a similar pair in cloth, and a pair of dressy shoes, but never for school.

"In the winter I wear this black thrift-shop skirt almost every day, with a shirt, a scarf around my neck, and a chain with little charms on it from friends. Or I'll wear jeans rolled up over my denim boots, a shirt with a thin sweater over it, and a scarf knotted at the neck.

"The black and Puerto Rican girls in school really pulled a look together that is sharp and very inexpensive. They'll wear earrings, a bracelet, a little hat, an inexpensive Indian cotton skirt, or rolled jeans with a thrift-shop jacket . . . and they look fabulous! It's not the budget, it's the imagination.

"On the weekends, I wear old school sweatpants with cowboy boots and a shirt. It's cheap, and it looks different!

"Sometimes I wish I had more money. I'd love to have clothes, but I don't want to own the same kind as the kids with money. Some of my things may look similar, but I think I always wear them differently."

ETHNIC

Ethnic clothes are in a certain disrepute these days. Lips curl at the mere sound of the word, and it's easy to understand why. Mass manufacturers have cheapened, bastardized, knocked off, diluted, and wrung the juice out of ethnic looks. And on top of all that, ethnic clothes have the gall to be bright and colorful in this depressed era of ours. But so what! Ethnic clothes can make you feel like a million bucks if you pick out the styles congenial to you. You can feel as if you're traveling to the Peruvian Andes as you set off for a business appointment; feel like you're off to a Hawaiian pig roast when you're actually en route to a leftover supper.

There's something about wearing a garment that's the product of another culture which is adventurous, even daring. If you have a beautiful printed silk kimono, for instance, you have to acclimate yourself to the bright, contrasting colors, to the sensual feel of the silk lining against your bare skin, the looseness of the sleeves and slit sides over a bare chest. You even have to move differently, because if you storm about a room in a normal Western way, your kimono will fall open. It gives you more body awareness—you quickly sense where your elbows are or you soon find the long, hanging arm of your kimono draped in the soup, in the salad, or up in flames.

The really special thing about ethnic

clothes is the fact that they are totally original. And when you blend in some exotic garment with your own well-worn and well-loved wardrobe, something interesting is bound to happen. (Just spend half an hour in your room with the radio blasting and start acquainting your new ethnic purchases with everything in your closet. You're sure to come up with a special look.) Ethnic clothes can be worn in a subtle way. They can be as classic as a tweed skirt if you think of them as individual garments rather than as parts of some exotic costume—if you take them out of context.

The trick of buying ethnic is to get a sense of the garment's inherent style and feel, independent of the rest of the outfit with which it's usually associated. Do with it what you will. Ethnic clothes seem to lose their vitality when foreign manufacturers move into a country and set up shop for mass-marketing designs that once had a very personal feel. After several years of these mass-manufactured imports, we have reached the point where we can select only the best. People are learning to look twice before they buy something with an ethnic air to it. It has to be a very special item; otherwise, you will be branded a hippy, and no one wants to look that dated! Selectivity pays off. In a few years, you won't be able to find true ethnic clothes anymore.

Sometimes it is easier to find national dress in the shops of America, like the Old Country stores along Clark Street in Chicago. A friend of ours was driving through Czechoslovakia several years ago and wanted to buy some typical Eastern European peasant scarves. There were none to be found in the bustling department stores of Prague. Yet, you can find them easily in New York. It seems that immigrant groups in the United States have held onto their national dress as a means of asserting their national identity; in the host country everyone rushes headlong into the future.

Lesley Jean Goldberg has made an art of the way she dresses, managing to put to-

The most elegant nomads of the Sahara desert are the Touareg tribe in Niger. Their loose robes, head wrappings, silver jewelry, embroidered money pouches and garments are all purchased at the market in Agades.

124

gether a very luxurious ethnic look without having the money to travel around the world. Lesley is an artist who works in soft sculpture, creating strange, attenuated people with looks of bland astonishment and plenty of sexual paraphernalia.

She assembled her beautiful wardrobe in San Francisco, where she haunted flea markets and used clothing shops, and cultivated friendships with the dealers who make trips to Africa, Asia, and the Near East. She has

Emmanuelle Khahn designed this graceful handkerchief skirt, the trim patiently embroidered by deft Roumanian artisans. Venitia finds it an ideal outfit for the squash court.

amassed so much jewelry that some hangs as decor in her house and the rest spills out of a big, beautiful Japanese mother-of-pearl chest. She has big, heavy Russian pieces, necklaces and coins, and silver and amber from Morocco, Ethiopia, Afghanistan, the Berbers, Turkomans . . . rare coral and enamels, carnelian, turquoise and jade rings, mammoth opalescent Dutch beads, African trade beads, Peking glass, ivory, carved blood-red cinnabar, bone and coral. She spends a lot of time at her collecting but pays very little for these very special pieces. She knows the value of things and has paid her dues learning where to get them.

Lesley has, she admits, more jewelry than clothes, but her favorite dresses carry out the ethnic style: a beautiful quilted-cotton Russian coat that she wears lining-out; a kimono found at a flea market that she re-cut into a loose V-necked dress because the edges were frayed. She loves soft silks and panne velvets, and when she's not wearing one of three extraordinary robes, Lesley puts her tops and dresses on over a long black velvet skirt and expensive boots, or mixes ethnic pieces with Victorian antiques. Lesley always looks like an exotic vision, a traveler back from Timbuktu loaded down with luxurious booty.

Martine Sitbon does travel. She says that dressing well is not a question of money. She doesn't buy ready-to-wear but looks for the special items that really please her. For about ten years she's dressed in old clothes from her grandmother's attic and thrift shops, but now she's turned her attention to antique ethnic clothes. "They're colorful and not sophisticated. I like a prophet look, large white Moses robes! I dream of Cecil B. DeMille movie clothes walking around, beautiful wool burnouses and big cotton djellabas. And I think make-up and kohl is important to accentuate a mood. I see it as an exaggeration, a kind of daily theatrics. Every day you wear a different mask. You put your mood on your face with makeup, and it, in turn, affects you and the people around you."

If you or one of your friends is about to take off on an exotic journey, here are a few observations and hints about the special finds you can discover while traveling.

Markets Around the World

Long before there were shopping centers and supermarkets, specialty stores and boutiques, goods were being traded in open or large covered markets. People gathered at regular intervals to buy, sell, trade, and gossip. The marketplace was the center of town as it still is in most country villages outside North America. Village markets in any country always seem to generate excitement. They are a feast for the eye as well as the place for cheap finds.

The first buy is a local **basket** or bag.

The Majorca/Ibiza straw basket is now an essential international summer carryall. Everyone who visits these islands off the Mediterranean coast of Spain buys one. The shape and flexibility of the basket are so practical that stores all over the world carry it as a steady item. In some countries the basket may turn out to be a net (like the *filet* in France), a knotted square of cotton from Japan, a stiff, round basket reinforced with metal shipping bands from Jamaica, or the goatskin bag of southern Morocco.

Make sure to find a light basket for long-distance trekking.

Markets are usually divided into stalls, and most of the time you will find the fruits and vegetables in one area, the meat and fish in another, and then an area for clothes, kitchen utensils, and crafts. The fabric and clothing sections are very different from market to market, depending on the abilities, ingenuity, and needs of the local people.

Each country and each province within that country has a set of traditions and clothes which by now take a trained eye to spot, since the whole world is becoming increasingly Westernized. People who like unusual clothes are quick to discover the find that is not imported at an enormous markup. Clothing sold at the marketplace may look attractive and colorful to the foreign eye, but it is there primarily because it is functional, durable, cheap, and usually made of local raw materials.

What to Look for in

EUROPE

Europe is the Old Country where fabric and color know-how originated. To learn how to recognize quality sweaters, for instance, step into a truly British shop and finger all the cashmere sweaters until you appreciate the difference between synthetics and the finest of wools. In France, Switzerland, and Italy, buy a yard or two of the most luxurious fabrics—crepe de Chine, georgette, or peau de soie—make a shift or wear it as a head scarf. If possible, always buy fabrics in the country of origin, where you get the advantage of local prices.

BRITAIN is famous for its quality sweaters. Shetland and lambs' wool can be found all over the country in chain stores and Woolworths at decent prices. Tweeds at all price levels are also a perennial item, particularly in Scotland, where weavers have a way of blending earthy colors that take your imagination back to the highlands. In Scotland the multitude of clan plaids sell by the kilt or by the yard.

IRELAND knits some of the warmest white wool sweaters on any side of the Atlantic Ocean. They are worn by everyone, whether they work the land, do office work, or simply pub crawl in Dublin. These sweaters are also perfect for the ski slopes of the Alps and Colorado, wintry campuses, and city streets.

SCANDINAVIA has all the best local clothes in the back country. The northern countries still have a strong folklore tradition which keeps local costumes dancing through the villages. In Norway, Sweden, and Finland, the country women wear white embroidered shirts with wide, embroidered, handwoven wool skirts over petticoats. They usually add a white apron and a bonnet (which we can do without today), but the tight, little, laced-up bolero completing the outfit is appealing. New ones can be found in the general stores and at local dressmakers, used ones in the secondhand shops. In Norway the best buys are the colorful sweaters with plain backgrounds and geometric patterns that start at the neck and expand toward the chest. They are sold as cardigans or crew necks, and if you have the time, they can be knitted for you in your own choice of colors if you can find a willing pair of hands.

Sweden excels in contemporary sports clothes, found in most of their department stores. There is a Swedish army coat which strikes many men visitors as being very practical. It's white canvas lined with sheepskin, with large pockets, and is cut, like all military clothes, with great classic proportions. The Swedish army coat can be found used in surplus stores or made new for a reasonable price at any military tailor. It looks good soiled, but if you like it white, wash it often in lukewarm water and let it dry away from direct heat.

GERMANY makes sturdy and efficient items without frivolities. The styles are often stiff, the colors muddy. Walking shoes are strong and well-made, but the Germanic forté is leather—coats and jackets that last a lifetime.

HOLLAND has its share of sailors' outfits, and Amsterdam has a "thieves' market" (or flea market) with a lot of good antique clothing.

BELGIUM: In no other place in the world are the women so agile with their fingers as the lacemakers in Ghent. Try replacing a worn collar with a dash of exquisite Belgian lace, or buy it by the yard to blend with other fabrics for a dress.

FRANCE, like the rest of Europe, has great local weekly markets where you can find things not sold in stores: slippers, wooden clogs with straw outside and sheepskin inside, large calico aprons, peasant blouses, long cotton underwear, head scarves, and fabrics that reflect the temperature of the region. Brittany has lots of rain; therefore you can be sure to find good sailors' raincoats and navy sweaters. The Riviera basks in the sun and produces the tiniest, best-cut bikinis in the world, as well as a whole array of light cotton sportswear in warm colors. Markets, small shoe stores, and department stores all carry the marvelous walking shoe known as "l'espadrille." It originated as a peasant shoe made with a canvas top and a light flexible straw from Algeria, ideal for weaving into a most comfortable sole.

French people have a knack for redesigning functional wear into appealing, must-have-it-in-your-wardrobe pieces of clothing. The espadrille became the most sensible footwear to own for men, women, and children. At first you could buy it only with a flat sole. Then Yves St. Laurent spotted a Basque shop near his first ready-to-wear store which handmade the shoes with an elevated wedge and laces to tie around the ankles. He contracted the Basque workshop to turn them out exclusively for his boutique. Flowers were embroidered on the canvas, and the colors became wilder until everyone caught on that the espadrille with an elevated heel was really the happiest and most comfortable shoe around. Now they are manufactured throughout the United States and Europe in a great variety of shapes and sizes. Chances are that you will not find a cheaper shoe except for the weird, functional sandal known as the "shrimping sandal," made of molded plastic.

SPAIN AND PORTUGAL both are a delight for people who have the patience and imagination to have their clothes custom-made. Ask around and someone is bound to recommend a good seamstress who will copy your favorite old shirt or whip up a skirt with hand finishing in the exact style you desire. Madrid was once famous for its suede and soft-leather shops that could custom-tailor anything you wanted in a few days. Now, as foreign manufacturers monopolize the market, there seem to be fewer shops like these. Yet the quality, color, and fit of the work of the small workshops and craftsmen found in Spain are very rewarding for people who love the feel of suede and leather. The Barrio Chino in Barcelona has the strongest boots (inspired by Frye) for a mere $25.00. In Majorca, ingenious cobblers make custom boots and shoes. Ordinary lace-up boots can be specially made with a small patch of Moroccan carpeting. If this costs more than your purse can afford, you can always pick up the best Spanish walking shoes—part canvas, part suede, with a sole made from recycled tires. Several people we know have been wearing them for four years or more. Pollensa in Majorca is one of the towns that specializes in this shoe. A similar style of sandal, locally called "Tijuana retreads," is available throughout the American Southwest at a very modest price.

ITALY is also crazy for shoes. There are shoe stores on every corner, and even the cheapest have great styles and colors, particularly in Milan. There seems to be more emphasis on men's wear in Italy. Good, cheap, and stylish suits can be found in many department stores.

CZECHOSLOVAKIA, HUNGARY, RUMANIA, AND POLAND are the places to look for hand embroidery on white cloth, meticulously sewn by diligent female hands. The tradition of hand embroidery began for filling trousseaus, but today these beautiful peasant clothes can be purchased in government stores and tourist shops.

YUGOSLAVIA still has a lot of folk crafts at fairly cheap prices which the local people take for granted. A good selection can be found in folklore stores and high-class souvenir shops similar to the shops in New York's East Village. These stores carry jewelry, costumes, luggage, and assorted crafts brought in by the peasants on market day. Farmers come from the villages surrounding the cities with sacks of knit socks, sandals woven from leather strips, vegetables, and cheeses for sale or trade. Mixed with all these goods are beautifully embroidered robes and intricate filigree bracelets that they regard as mere old clothing and trinkets. Bartering and trading between visitor and peasant is quite popular, especially when done with a smile and for the pleasure of the exchange.

Large cotton muslin peasant scarves can be worn many ways: babushka style, wrapped as a turban, tied as a halter or beach skirt. From Greece or Greek stores.

GREECE has, from time immemorial, seen its people dressed in shirts and dresses made from the off-white gauze that is woven on the islands. In the days of Socrates, the cloth was worn as a toga, and today it seems that summer clothes are returning to these loose, comfortable styles. Once again the mills are

weaving the white cloth that is so perfect for wrapping and draping. After you have covered your body, choose an open pair of sandals which slip around your toe. The Greeks really know how to make sandals that last, as well as using the prettiest colors for decoration. Jewelry found in Greece is particularly attractive and can run from the simple bronze cross of Mikonos to the bright blue glass beads taken from donkeys' saddles and strung into necklaces.

Russian peasant clothes: the woman's dress of the Ryazan province; the man's traveling coat is from central Russia.

RUSSIA is one of the few countries where amber is in abundance. Necklaces, bracelets, and rings can be purchased very reasonably at Beryoskas in the government shops catering to tourists who will pay in foreign currency. Another sound buy is the Chapka, that famous Russian hat with the ear flaps. Made of mink tails, fox, astrakhan, or rabbit fur, they will keep any head warm even in the coldest of Siberian winters. If you do go as far as Siberia, track down the secondhand shops—with luck you may find a local policeman's sheepskin coat in off white or brown. The superb tailoring, the fitted chest, and large collar make them very special.

The most Russian of all garments is the side-fastening, collarless, bloused shirt worn in khaki wool by the army and in beige/brown by the country people. The festive version of these shirts is made in white or black satin with embroidered ribbons at the cuff and neck, held loosely at the waist with a wide leather belt or a simple cord. The image of traditional Russia is that of a country woman wearing a long jacket over a loose dress with heavy boots, her head covered with a babushka or floral scarf of wool challis with pink and red roses mingled in among green leaves.

AFRICA

This is a continent where you can sit for hours at the marketplace with the robe maker and discuss at length the blue of a cloth, the zigzag designs his machine can perform, and describe what you want for yourself by indicating what you like on the people passing by. Most of the population in countries like Algeria, Morocco, Tunisia, Mali, Niger, and Egypt have been wearing the same basic type of clothing for the past two thousand years: pre–New Testament classics such as woven woolen capes that double as blankets, gabardine caftans, and large cotton robes for both men and women.

NORTH AFRICA is one of the least bastardized of all regions as far as clothes are concerned. The *souk* is the old open market of the large towns. You're well advised to take one of those self-appointed guides that crowd the entrance, because the place is like a labyrinth. These guides are usually young boys full of tricks and enthusiasm. Select the calmest one you can find since they can drive you crazy trying to make dizzy deals with their store-owner companions (to whom they will no doubt lead you at triple speed). You can wander in alone, but you'll find that all along the way young boys will walk alongside of you whether you like it or not. Once you see

These Moroccan women adorn themselves with their finest amber and silver jewelry. The huge, inlaid metal triangles add beauty but also secure veil and robe against the mountain winds. Silver kohl accents their eyes.

something you really want, you might as well get it right there, because you are going to see hundreds that look pretty much alike, and the few pennies you might bargain down are not worth the energy. Or, you can choose your cloth and trimmings for a *djellaba* (a long house robe) and go over all the details with the tailor: length of sleeve, side slits, etc. All this usually takes place over a cup of sweet mint tea. Shopping in Arab countries is considered an agreeable pastime; you meet, sit, chat, and exchange views. It is not an impersonal

Ever wonder how all the ethnics come together? Here's an English wool cap, Scotch cashmere sweater, tightly woven and patterned African bag, worn with traditional American blue jeans, legwarmers (they date back to the Ballet Russe), and snazzy midcalf cowboy boots!

supermarket or department-store operation where you dash in, grab, pay, and dash out.

EQUATORIAL AFRICA has body coverings, for the bush and cities alike, that are even more basic. The wide, loose shirts for men let the air through and can be bought at the market in a great variety of prints. The women wrap their heads with a large piece of cotton batik and wrap their bodies from bosom to ankles in a similar print. At the market you can get typically colorful African batiks with cameos of the local president or the late President Kennedy, General de Gaulle, and other political personalities.

In any country, check what the local people are wearing on their feet; it's usually the cheapest and most durable regional footwear. In this part of the world shoes are called *samsaras*, and can be found at the stall of the man in charge of leather at the general market. The same vendor will also have leather pouches worn around the neck or diagonally across the chest, which serve as a money purse for both men and women. These hand-sized pouches are worked in different-colored leathers and have many concealed compartments to store amulets, money, medicinal herbs, and photographs.

Venetian beads used centuries ago as bartering pieces, and no longer available in Venice, pile up in little mounds of swirling colors among the heavy silver bracelets in the alleyways. The blanket vendors sell carefully woven narrow strips stitched together to form assorted-sized blankets with geometric patterns and dazzling colors. If you arrive early at the bush or city market, you can get everything at almost half price —a friendship discount. Ideally, one should not require any other entertainment, because the open markets are so fantastic. As the heart and life of any region, they give you a real feeling for the country. In Nigeria and Ghana the heavy-work laborers wear a cotton patchwork sleeveless tunic that sells for less than 50¢.

All over Africa, the most venerated man next to the local chief and the medicine man is the blacksmith. He not only makes horseshoes but also fashions silver jewelry out of coins by melting and casting them in sand.

Henna-mud designs, lasting for two weeks to a month, both decorate and antisepticize. These designs took an entire day of skillful and ancient craftsmanship.

In Agades, Niger, we saw a European woman, amazed at the timeless, precise work of the blacksmith, give him one of her favorite Navajo bracelets to copy. The result was all the more interesting since it combined two very distinct and distant cultures.

A great part of the Niger population consists of the Tuareg or "blue people," who wrap their heads in a navy blue fabric that looks like carbon paper. The color from the fabric rubs off on their heads, which is the reason why they are called blue people. They are a nomadic tribe who roam the area carrying goods to inaccessible regions. A rugged people, they have for centuries worn loose, wide robes and turbans to resist heat, wind, and sand. The women gracefully wrap yardage of azure blue cloth above a long robe of white lace. When they have children, the long robe is cut at the waist so the baby can be breast fed. These people have become such masters at artfully using fabric that during the dawn dance they manage to make their headgear resemble a cock's comb, the animal they want to imitate.

Another nomadic tribe of that country are the Fulani. The men and women wear little pouches around their necks that contain small mirrors and a pair of tweezers to remove both the thorns from their feet and the hair from their foreheads and beards.

All over Africa, there is an endless variety of beadwork and the use of grass or straw for skirts, hats, and bags. Besides the marketplace, there are talented craftspeople who work in small huts tucked away in villages. If you can express what it is you are looking for, the local people will lead you to the artisans.

THE MIDDLE EAST

This area has a very limited selection of women's wear, except for the big white sheet exposing only one eye. (But you just might go for an Arafat type of head wrap.) Men are equally uniformed, in their long white robes and muslin turbans.

TURKEY has deep red velvet jackets and dresses which have gotten even better with age. They are often embroidered with gold or silver threads and can be retrieved from masses of smelly clothes in Ali Baba-type secondhand shops. Turkey is also well known for beautiful silver belts which, depending on the source and workmanship, run from about $40 to $300. Local shops in Istanbul and in many little villages display crinkled cotton shirts in a natural egg-shell color, with or without red stripes. The same garment can be found in knee or ankle length and are all very cheap.

JORDAN AND ISRAEL have the Bedouin woman's dress with the embroidered yoke, one of the most sensible long robes on earth. It comes in either heavy cotton or black velvet and is tucked under the breast all the way to the waist. When a woman reaches the middle of a pregnancy, it is untucked for extra room.

PAKISTAN AND AFGHANISTAN have been overexploited for their mirror-embroidered

Baby stays snug in this little Afghanistan mirrored coat straight from the market-place in the mountains.

skirts and shirts, and the strong-smelling goatskin coats. Yet the women who live in the northern regions wear a type of clothing very different from that seen in the south. They are difficult to see because the women hide themselves behind a black veil with only a net insert at eye level, but underneath they wear large black cotton dresses with silver embroidery of great beauty, worn with heavy silver bangles. If you love boots and want to have a pair made that will be inexpensive but very special, see the cobblers of Afghanistan, who work in leather and make soft riding boots that can be ordered with or without embroidery.

INDIA has such a huge selection of cheap clothes that one really has to examine carefully before buying. The rush was so great on all the long cotton skirts, vests, Nehru type shirts and such that little attention was given to the quality of the stitching or the cut. However, the people of India who still care produce some of the finest clothes such as the very popular *kurta* (white voile shirts with simple drawstring pants). Each province of India has an individual style—the state of Baroda, the state of Madras, and so on, each with particular colors and prints for the saris in which the women wrap themselves.

KASHMIR, the fertile and lush valley at the top of India, is a paradise for market lovers. It is the kingdom of papier-mâché—beautiful jewelry and jewelry boxes, painted with intricate miniature floral designs and then varnished to sparkle in the sun. Fur coats abound, but again, if you have one made, select the skins with someone who is knowl-

edgeable. The hides should be supple, the fur shiny. Work closely with the tailor so that the seams are not half done with weak thread and the length is correct, as Americans in general are considerably taller than the local inhabitants. Wolf, fox, and other skins can be made into coats for about $100. Embroidered shawls made of the finest wools come in subtle shades and are covered with hand-stitched paisley designs.

NEPAL, the small country that begins where India rises to meet the Himalaya Mountains, has quilted coats of heavy hand-woven fabrics that can be dyed and/or made to order. People there have a wonderfully unique way of layering colorful woolen garments when the cold sets in.

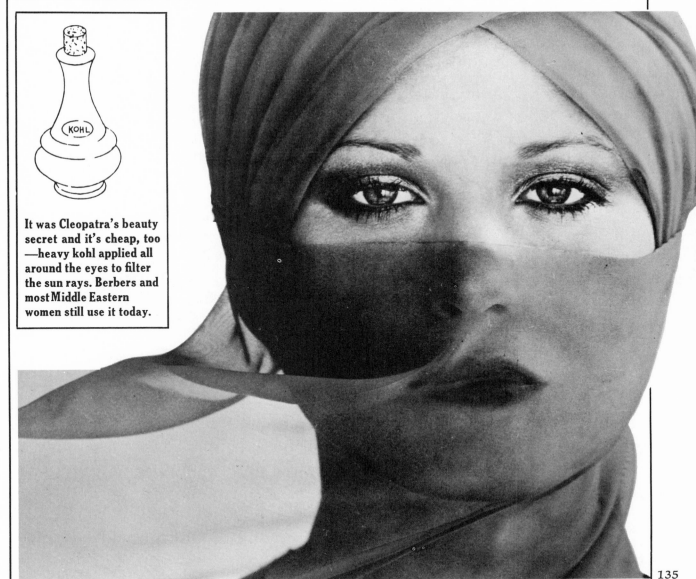

It was Cleopatra's beauty secret and it's cheap, too—heavy kohl applied all around the eyes to filter the sun rays. Berbers and most Middle Eastern women still use it today.

ASIA

As you will discover in the wrapping chapter, INDONESIA has developed maximum simplification in its clothes. Men and women wear a sarong or length of waxed batik wrapped around the hips as a long skirt. For women it is topped with a sheer voile, loose blouse edged with flower embroidery.

In BALI, the graceful and magical island, the young boys walk along the beaches with dried seaweed bracelets, delicate shell necklaces, and tortoiseshell rings. To find the best bargains in batiks, go deep into the market, as the peripheral vendors are out to get the hurried tourist for as much as they can. (For those who like pipes, the Balinese are also great carvers of ebony or bone pipes, chiseled with great love and artistry.)

When we think of Bali, we think of Dorothy Lamour, revealing sarongs, and the irresistible lure of strong, tropical perfume. We can't provide the Lamour or the perfume, but here are a few hints about the cotton sarong or pareo wraps. Cotton is the best natural fiber in a hot and humid climate because it allows the body to breathe freely. The best cotton now seems to be coming from mainland China. The most beautifully batiked designs are layered by hand, using one color at a time. Hot wax prevents it from going where it isn't wanted (thus the term *wax resist*). The delicate, sophisticated patterns are created layer by layer in a slow painstaking process. A very complex and fine piece of work can take as long as a year, just like the creation of a fine, handwoven Japanese obi. Some of the typical patterns are Kawung (simple geometrics that look like colliding amoebae); Parong (diagonal squiggled stripes); Three Countries (a patchwork); Magamundum (the Chinese Cloud of Life); and Pekalongan (an exotic floral design incorporating the most complex wax-resist process).

The Chinese influence on European dress is spreading fast. Stylish Parisian Sofi Bollack picked out this old black and gold brocade and had it transformed into a classic coat-dress.

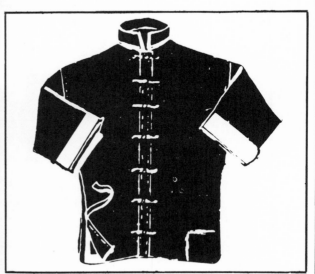

This basic kung-fu attire can also be an everyday jacket.

HONG KONG, Taiwan's neighbor, requires looking beyond the typical tourist traps to discover the really cheap and useful finds. There is a five-story building on the main street of the island called the China Em-

Kansai: Euro-Japanese design at its most exuberant. 137

Designer Betsey Johnson (read about her on page 185) goes to Hong Kong regularly on designing trips. Advice from her last visit? Almost everything is gone! Yue-ha is the best store—a department store chock full of mainland Chinese goods. The zappiest custom-made shoes and boots can be had for $30 to $60 if you know what you want!

porium which sells a great assortment of quality goods made in mainland China. It is an outlet for them to collect foreign currency, and the prices on most things are extremely reasonable. A friend of ours bought a backpack embroidered with funny animals which was a solid combination of silk and cotton. For her boyfriend, she brought back a navy blue quilted jacket which is as warm as a fur coat.

The "Chinese blues" are everywhere, of course. Both men and women wear those loose pants and straight jackets with frog fastenings. Depending on your inclination, you can get them either ready-made there or in any Chinatown in your own country. In Hong Kong you can pick up a smooth navy blue velvet jacket with silk lining and give it to a local tailor, who will quilt and custom finish it with special frogs in just a few days for about the same price as a jean's jacket and dungarees at home.

In China the regime of Mao brought about a sobriety in fashion which is very much in line with the Cheap Chic utilitarian idea. Yet there is a great deal of beauty and charm in the ancient Chinese robes, long skirts, and pajamas that are still worn today

by older people in Hong Kong, Taiwan, and Chinese communities abroad. The amazing fact is that a lot of these decorated coat dresses can still be purchased at reasonable prices all over the world; they make most attractive at-home or party wear.

JAPAN

JAPAN is a treasure trove for anyone who appreciates refinement and delicacy in color and print. All the energy concerning clothes has gone into the same basic form for hundreds of years, the kimono. The only difference in kimonos lies in the fabric. The very formal way for a Japanese woman to dress is first to wear a knee-length white cotton kimono belted loosely with a length of dyed silk. On top of that goes a kimono of thin silk or rayon in a pastel color (usually printed with cherry blossoms) tied with an even more elaborate sash, then the final kimono of a color and embroidery dictated by the occasion. The formal kimono is truly an art form in itself, with paintings depicting an aspect of nature stitched in a world of glori-

Japanese designer Kansai Yamamoto's dramatic cape.

ously colored threads. The large sash or *hobi* securing the top kimono is carefully considered and almost as costly as the kimono because of the handwoven brocade from which it is made.

For everyday wear, the outer kimono for both men and women is of a flat woven cotton or wool in earthy tones, often with a geometric pattern discreetly running through the fabric. For our money, the *yukata* is the most accessible and practical kimono. It is worn by the Japanese either at home or for traveling to and from the bath house. It usually comes in white cotton printed with natural or abstract motifs in navy blue or mauve. In a spa town you will see everyone walking around in these robes, and it is a refreshing sight. The *yukata* can be purchased for about $10 in any Japanese department store or for slightly more in the Japanese stores in our country.

A variation of these house kimonos is the *hoppi* coat, most often seen in black with a good-luck symbol or dragon on the back. Another very practical Japanese invention are *zoris*, or thong sandals, which come in every form—flat, on stilts, with straw soles, with a cork platform, with velvet or plastic padding. The *tabi*, or white cotton foot covering that fastens on the side, completes the traditional wear. It is fairly inexpensive, but not very practical. Nippon ingenuity also includes beautiful but cheap waxed paper umbrellas priced so that you don't mind losing it.

A Nippon oil-paper umbrella serves well in America to protect this southern belle from the sun.

SOUTH AMERICA

Throughout South America there is a general feeling for simple hand-woven cloth that has multiple uses. The Indians turn out the most interesting combinations of colors and textures.

MEXICO, the sad and singing country that touches its white cotton clothes with vibrant colors, still produces a lot of attractive, cheap clothing. The market of Toluca, not far from Mexico City, sells a huge assortment of shiny, multicolored scarves.

Natural cotton is egg-shell colored. The shirts of this material that most men wear on Sundays in the villages are sold in the markets. They have long sleeves, narrow

This Mexican jacket of embroidered white wool goes for $25 in Paris, which is probably triple its price in Mexico.

pleats, and tiny bone or plastic buttons. In the south of Mexico, where it gets hotter, women's dresses are looser, like chemises, with large flowers embroidered on the shoulder straps and front to resemble big necklaces. Walking for long distances in the dusty heat is a part of life there, and the famous *huaraches*, leather-strip sandals, developed out of that need. Their flexibility and airiness have also made them very popular abroad.

Each country in South America has its distinct, almost national, sweater. In Mexico, the most appealing and classic is of thick natural wool with a shawl collar that comes up to your ears to protect your neck from the cold at night. Silver jewelry is cheap and looks it, but it is fun and imaginative. There are all sorts of brooches in butterfly or bird shapes, outlined in silver and inlaid with iridescent abalone shells, and small perfume bottles covered with cut-out silver flowers that let you see the remaining level of the liquid. You may find a *mariachi* leather belt studded with shiny nails, or an armadillo bag, which is both a curious and rather sad object.

GUATEMALA follows much the same line of clothing as its Mexican neighbor, except that the ponchos and shawls are even more common and often become a skirt, a scarf, or a head wrap at the twist of a wrist. You'll discover that each town has its own distinct weaving colors.

BRAZIL is so widespread and varied that it is difficult to pinpoint the many local specialties. The general markets are called *feiras*. In the cities they move to a different section every day. In the beach towns like Rio, you can purchase mercerized cotton thread at one stand, hand it over to be crocheted at the next stand, and have a bikini the next day for approximately $8. As an alternative to T-shirts, you can get some of those skimpy, spaghetti-strapped undershirts; they are made of cotton and take well to dyeing. A tougher look is that of the *cangaceiros*, the cowboys of Brazil, who wear all-leather chaps and tight jackets worn with wide sombrero hats. The saddle makers also produce large bags of different kinds of leathers. The prettiest and least expensive hot-weather clothes come from the region of Bahia. Men of all ages wear white cotton trousers and loose white blouses in the Macumba region. Women's skirts are long, extremely wide, and often trimmed with lace.

People in Brazil pay a great deal of attention to superstition, and many will carry a few charms to ward off evil spirits. The most popular one is the *figa*, a carved hand with the thumb stuck between the index and the next finger. You can find them for very little money, made out of the semiprecious stones that abound in Brazil.

The Amazon Indians have a way of weaving fine straw and dyeing feathers to create tickly necklaces. They also alternate beans, dipped in earthy colors, with little stones and tinted feathers, as is done nowhere else in the world.

BOLIVIA AND PERU have very colorful ponchos, gloves, and bonnets, knit with child-like designs, which keep the mountaineers warm and free in their movement. Whenever a traveler starts talking about the markets of South America, the conversation always comes back to the multitude of patterns in weaving. It is also an amazing sight to see women at the market wearing hats that closely resemble bowlers or businessmen's hats.

More booty from Mexico is this handpainted sequined skirt. Only sixteen dollars across the border!
Right, The South American Mix: A Mexican blanket skirt, Bolivian sweater and a coat from a Peruvian poncho.

CATALOGUE HITS

In the last few years, there has been a virtual explosion in the shopping-at-home field. There are catalogues for every occasion; items for every persuasion. The big three, J. C. Penney, Sears Roebuck and Company, and Montgomery Ward, offer an exciting new array of both fashionable clothes and transformable goodies like old-lady slips you can dye and make into summer dresses; painter's pants; and all sorts of work clothes. Each catalogue has a different requirement for getting on the mailing list, but often, if you order by mail from one, you will find yourself suddenly receiving catalogues from all the others. This can be either a blessing or —if you're on a tight budget—a curse. Some of these catalogues offer such enticing items it's hard not to send right off for them. Also, technological innovation has reared its lovely head among catalogues, and there are many, including staid L. L. Bean, that offer 800-code (toll-free) long-distance calls. You simply pick up your phone and dial in your order. Charge it, of course. Many take Master Charge, VISA, and American Express. And since merchandise is returnable, shopping by mail can be a real convenience for working women who like to spend weekends relaxing (and don't consider shopping on Saturday a mode of relaxation).

THE BIG ONES

Since all catalogues change each season (or, in the case of the smaller ones, every few months) the specific items shown on these pages may no longer be available as you read this book. But we show them to give you a taste of the

143

kind of clothes—both fashion, and fashion-in-disguise—you can turn up in the pages of these catalogues. . . .

Here are some tempting items from **J. C. Penney's** catalogue. As mentioned in the first chapter, it's smart to buy clothes in multiples, choosing solid colors that make sense with what you already have in your wardrobe. Penney has interesting tank tops in strong solids like green, yellow, blue, ivory, and orange, at approximately $6. They come with matching drawstring pants. Classic T-shirts in pastels with cap sleeves go for the same price. They're good with skirts, or match them up with sports shorts with elasticized waists.

For wrapping, you can even get a pareo from Penney, with a matching bikini. Tie it at the hip or, to make a strapless dress for evening, around the bust.

Get their really sexy bikini (with top and bottom sold separately) and suit the style perfectly to *your* figure.

The leotards are shiny Antron and Lycra. They make nice maillots for swimming or exercise leotards when worn with tights.

Penney has a classic man-style shirt with a turn-up collar that looks great belted over a skirt—and it's machine washable as well. Or order directly from their men's pages for a really loose fit.

The "Savvy" section of the Penney catalogue says "you understand that understatement is elegant." If understated elegance is *your* understanding of style, this section might be for you.

And when you want to get away from it all, you can order a great big beautiful bed with linens designed by Cathy Hardwick—a terrific clothing designer—in soft watercolor pastels with lots of feminine flounces.

Night-time fashions from Penney's: you can sleep in the nude and still be well-dressed.

144

Montgomery Ward's Rita Perna, assistant vice president and national fashion coordinator, says "the dress is having its day. It's bringing the leg out of hiding with one continuous flow of fabric or matching skirt and top." Ward has a pretty, crystal-pleated dress in Arnel for under $40—the neckline can be worn either on or off the shoulder. This dress, like many of the big three catalogue clothes, comes in talls, and many come in half sizes as well.

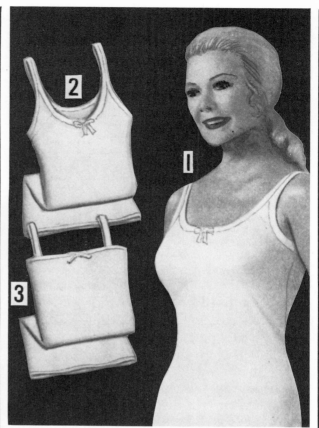

Ward's old-time undies: fabulous finds.

Also available is a beautiful shimmering Lycra four-way bandeau-look maillot bathing suit in a peacock blue that will knock your eyes out.

Ward's has equally enticing lingerie, but Cheap Chicers will enjoy rooting around in the back pages for items like the "straight-top vest" with a drawstring around the neckline and ribbon straps, just right for dyeing. (They also come with matching bloomers. In pink only.)

There are also cute "cuff panties" in pink acetate that must have been first offered around 1933.

The one-piece underwear is always comfy for wearing around the house, and the enterprising accessorizer could, undoubtedly, wear it around town with impunity, once dyed and disguised!

Rockford socks are classics and look great with mules: their little red heels show on the tweedy brown and beige ground of the socks. (They also look awfully nice with traditional pink ballet slippers on sultry summer weekends in the country, perhaps with an old slip dyed a dusky pink.)

You'll go ape over these socks. Cool, comfortable cotton with bright red heels to perk up your footsies.

"Cotton utility hose" are another Ward's find. They're *seamed* fine cotton in beige or taupe, three pairs for under $8. Just the thing for the Virginia Woolf look.

The men's work clothes section has a lot of intriguing items, like the fourteen-pocket canvas apron and the leather, two-bag carpenter's apron. The fourteen-pocket canvas apron might be just the ticket for free-lance photojournalists who cart around lots of cameras and film.

Sears Roebuck offers "designer groups" where two or so pieces work together as classics, like the outfit shown above. This soft lamb's wool, angora, and nylon sweater, tattersall shirt and tweed jacket, worn with pleated pants or skirt and handsome boots.

Their man's "shop coat" makes a perfect white summer coat with three big pockets, a snap-front closing, and side slits, all for around $12. You can also find "shop aprons" that are great for cooking.

If your look is more feminine, try their camisole and petticoat of eyelet embroidery. They're not 100 percent cotton, so you'd have to consult your local dime-store expert to see if Rit Dye will take.

Sears Western Catalogue has things like leather thongs, handwoven Indian-style blankets of reused wool (they make great rugs), and wide, mohair girths you can make into huge belts. They also sell handsome straight-leg chaps made of cowhide, buckstitched in white with a fringed trim.

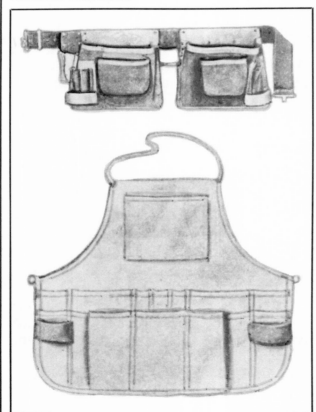

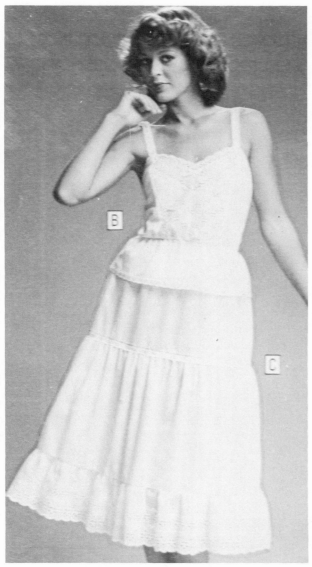

From super-macho leathers to super-feminine lace, Sears has got the goods.

SOME SMALL ONES

The smaller catalogues range from the outdoor chic of L. L. Bean in Maine, Fulton Supply Company in New York, or I. Goldberg & Company in Philadelphia, to the high style of store catalogues like I. Magnin's or Bonwit Teller's. Here are just a few examples. Again, they're only representative of the kind of thing you might find. By the time you read this, most of the merchandise will have moved on. . . .

Trifles is a new catalogue from Horchow. For example, a soft gray dress with white collar and cuffs works any season, over a turtleneck, under a vest. They also have all sorts of lovely gifts, an enticement to give *yourself* gifts!

Viva Magazine Products sells really sexy lingerie through the mail, in case you'd rather not buy it in person, like this tiny Antron bra trimmed with scroll lace and matching bikini with teeny satin bows.

Frederick's of Hollywood has fabulous marabou-trimmed stilettos, springolator-style, in black, white, candy pink, powder blue, hot pink, red, or champagne. They're called Glamour Doll, and they're hard to find on Main Street!

Brownstone Studio offers classics especially useful for the working woman. We found this nice Anne Klein belt there, in good basic colors.

147

Sakowitz has a cunning catalogue that makes you feel you're about to read a fascinating magazine. Since their store is based in Houston, you'll find lots of things good for a warm climate, like a gorgeous raw silk, rolled-sleeve shirt with a shirred yoke, and gathered dirndl-waist pants with a narrow leg . . . both in a creamy ivory.

Chris-Craft is for the sporty life, offering lots of electronic gear as well as athletic gear. Their warm-up suit is in sweatshirt gray with bright red at the neck closure, and it comes in men's sizes as well. You can also find their rainbow-bright Chris-Craft Maine-style moccasins and boots, great for the out-of-doors, and hot sellers in Manhattan's most fashionable stores.

Adam York offers a heavy-duty tool bag of ten-ounce natural canvas with leather handles, straps, and reinforcements. You could probably get it cheaper by tracking it down at a supply store, but the catalogue offers the convenience of ordering by mail or toll-free call . . . and charging!

Kaleidoscope, out of Atlanta, offers special clothes suited for warm climes and very special gifts. These tank-watch faces are in white, red, or green acrylic with real lizard straps. They look great with sportswear.

Crafty Chris-Craft warms up the gray warm-up suit with a touch of red at the neck.

Norm Thompson promises an "escape from the ordinary," and offers all sorts of Oregonian outdoor delights. Classic tailoring, subtle colors, and high-quality natural fabrics make these a sure bet. They may not be cheap, but they'll last you a lifetime.

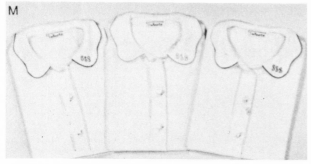

The Talbot's, from Hingham, Massachusetts, is instant Ivy League by mail. Where else could you find these monogrammed scalloped-collar blouses shown above in bright, innocent white with bluebell, hot-pink, green, red, navy, or yellow trim? Or the monogrammed crewneck Shetland sweater? You can find the sweaters for men here also.

The chic-est initials are your own, when they're monogrammed on this sweater from The Talbots.

The Horchow Collection was the first catalogue to merchandise a collection of exclusive, big-city status possessions like Rigaud scented candles, Cartier tank watches, Tiffany key rings, or Givenchy loungewear, and make them available to every U.S. citizen by mail. Definitely the catalogue for the sensuous shopper. And that toll-free number! You can call up until 10:00 P.M., Texas time, so those late-night impulses can be instantly gratified. You could call right up and order something like a $325.00 Georg Jensen 17-jewel watch with a totally blank chrome face. For an extra $16.50 you can get a one-inch-wide brown pigskin band. Otherwise, you'll just have to settle for the flat black, which isn't bad. . . .

Sportpages is outdoor chic all the way. For winter, terrific suede after-ski boots; for summer, all sorts of nifty terry and velour bikinis, robes, and overshirts. Plus tennis gear up one side and down the other, like a Diane von Furstenberg velour knit sweatshirt in glowing sapphire.

Propinquity, from Los Angeles, had our favorite lamp, Gladys Goose, for everyone who is still a child at heart! And for those of you who still smoke (shame!) a classic WWI oval-ended lighter that buyers always end up giving away to admiring friends.

So . . . have fun with the catalogues, and try to watch that 800-hot-line-itch.

149

GERALDINE STUTZ

President of Henri Bendel

"Everyone has an individual style. It can be born of all things, including necessity," says Gerry Stutz, the only woman president of a major fashion department store in the U.S. Necessity, in this case, is Henri Bendel, New York's most chic specialty store for women. Gerry Stutz's magnificent and unique feel for the look that's just beyond now encourages her special blend of individual styles to coexist at Bendel's.

"Fashion says, 'me too,'" says Gerry Stutz, "and style says 'only me.' It's your way of saying HERE I AM. . . ." At Henri Bendel, the only "look" you'll find will be your own, because Miss Stutz wants it that way. She saw today's woman coming years ago, and that woman was herself. Bendel's reflects Gerry Stutz's special attitudes about style.

"The way it was before with fashion, you really felt that to look right, you had to move to the new 'look' each and every season. What happens now is that a woman gets tired of wearing the same thing, and she moves, by herself, to change it. What we're involved in now is a time when women are becoming more self-conscious, thinking about themselves as special, unique, one-of-a-kind . . . and that's got to be how they look, too.

"What were once the focal points of fashion, big things like skirt lengths, are now only a matter of proportion. Pants, for instance, may seem more interesting narrow, but only because women become bored. Not because the fashion press or some designer says, 'JUMP,' and snaps his fingers.

"Do you know how a designer designs a collection today? By asking around about what women are going to want. They try to get inside women's heads! That explains the emergence of so many more interesting women designers, who are really reading their own minds. They design for themselves, and they pick up fans the way guys cannot. Because women who are that style identify with the designer's image of herself. As it moves toward less fashion and more style, women designers are more apropos. Sonia Rykiel designs not just for style, but perfectly for shapes: her body is shaped like mine. There's Rykiel, Chantal Thomass, Norma Kamali, Mary McFadden, Carol Horn, Donna Karan, Harriet Winter, Pinky and Dianne, and lots more!"

"So while a woman wants to be herself, she's immediately drawn to a style that's like her own self-image. She looks at the dame and says, 'Eh, that's like me!' And if the designer is good, she moves along and keeps up the momentum. Women are moving fashion today, not the other way around!

"I'm in the process of putting together my four 'uniforms' for the year. It takes time and energy. Effort is the sine qua non in dressing yourself. Style, even if it doesn't seem to, demands effort. A person with style and no effort can look just dreadful. There are people with a really clear, sharp sense of communicating themselves. I think

Barbra Streisand was the first contemporary watershed for looking like yourself. Style is talent, like writing or performing, and the more training, the more polished the style becomes. It improves with exercise. It takes work.

"Each season I pull together four things —two remakes from my closet, and two new ones. I put all my attention, effort, and energy into altering them so they fit me perfectly, together with the right accessories. I'm a perfectionist about details. I've never believed that anything goes . . . never have . . . never will."

151

WRAPPINGS

Wrapping the body is the simplest form of clothing and the most sophisticated. Some people consider the clothes of classic Greece to be the height of elegance. Today, millions of people around the world wear pieces of cloth draped and knotted and folded about the body. In Southeast Asia, men and women wear identical sarongs. In Africa, Masai tribesmen throw a large piece of orange cloth over their shoulders like a dashing cape. Desert robes and intricate turbans protect the Arabs from heat, wind, and sand. On the Indian continent, women wear a long length of fabric wrapped about their body, a sari. In South America, Indians only twenty miles from large cities still wear the simple loincloth. In America, Zuni women wrap fabric into skirts.

The art of keeping a piece of fabric on your body shows in the way you pull it, tie it, and work with the tucks and folds and bias . . . there are no buttons or zippers. For those of us who grew up knowing nothing but fastenings and more fastenings—zips, buttons, hooks, eyes, snaps, and laces—it

All it takes to gift-wrap yourself is a certain assurance about preventing that piece of fabric from slipping off your body. Christiana's discovery is to make a triangle out of a large Indian silk scarf, then with the long edge up, cross it in back and knot the points in front. Add a silver belt to determine the waistline, a whisp of point d'esprit tulle at the neck for drama and you have ingenious evening wear for next to nothing.

may be rather difficult to relax wearing just a flimsy piece of fabric wrapped between our bodies and the cold, cold world. But once you start playing with the idea of wrappings, it can become very exciting. All you have to work with is:

The fabric
The body
Your imagination

A combination of these three things can become the most sensual thing ever! What painting is more sumptuous than Ingre's *Turkish Bath*? How sparse it would look without the full, intricately wrapped turbans on the heads of the naked bathers. Draped fabric offers a soft, charming look in this world of stiffness and neatness.

Wrap up a skirt and halter, if you find yourself really down and out. You'll be back on top of the world looking totally unique. No one will mix patterns and colors the way you do, no one is going to wrap their body just the way you do, and no one has a

For a sexy summer skirt, take a large fringed shawl, hug it tight around the hips and knot it below the belly-button. If the fabric is slippery, add a safety pin underneath for security (and peace of mind).

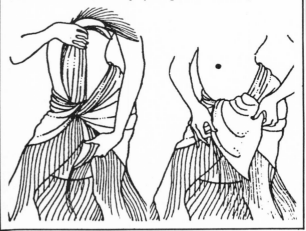

A sarong is traditional for men in Southeast Asia. It's as simple as a wrap around the hips, pull and tuck.

During her pregnancy, Marcia found the most comfortable covering around the house was a loosely held length of sari.

body to reveal that is quite like yours. You can't make a mistake. Wrapping is totally individual.

A girl who lives in Los Angeles makes full use of the warm weather—she pulls a long piece of peach jersey out of her drawer, wraps it once or twice around her body, plays with it this way and that, and finally settles on one style of draped gown for the evening. She has a talent for it, yes, but it's something we can all develop.

If you grow fond of this gentle, feminine look, you can buy yards and yards of silky jersey, Indian cotton muslin, antique scarves, Liberty of London prints, Provençal cottons, and Balinese saris; fabrics that stick to the body and don't slide around.

When you travel, pack a few folded lengths of fabric to soften modern motel lamps, change the color of the lighting, cover ugly bedspreads, hang as wispy curtains, and double up as beach towels and bikini covers. A few pieces of fabric can

The Bikini

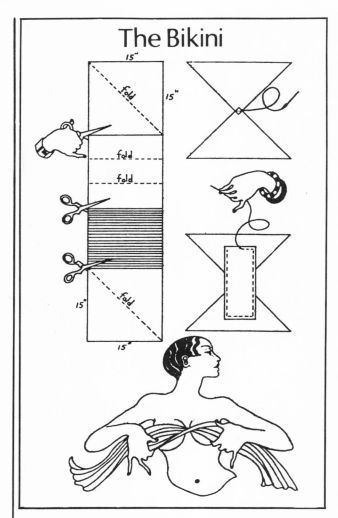

transform the mood of the grimmest institutional room—suddenly it looks personal and creative. You can do the same thing at home for a quick change of mood.

Inventive European models with little money soon develop a knack for finding bits and pieces to make into little, wrapped creations to express their very personal esthetic sense. Christiana Steidten always carries scarves to wrap into a strapless dress, a little bandeau top, or a floaty skirt, as you can see in the photographs.

There are endless ways of doing yourself up in fabric. To start, you might buy a three-yard length of light Indian cotton gauze, the best size for beginners. Take a look at the pictures in this section and start right in, twisting, tying, and tucking. One of the easiest skirts to create is copied from the Balinese. A three-yard length is wrapped

It's silly that the tiniest bikinis fetch ridiculous prices when it is so simple to create your own. It's just a twist of a wrist and two scarves. The ones shown here are 58 by 15 inches. For the bottom, cut the scarf on the solid line and fold on the dotted lines to make the back and front triangles. Fold the remaining material in thirds to make a long rectangle which is stitched in as the crotch; tie the corners at the hips and you have bikini pants. For the top use a similar scarf, same size, twist it in the center and tie snugly in back or at the neck.

What do you do when the occasion calls for a dress and all you've got is jeans? Christiana, like most models, doesn't even bother with dresses. But she has developed the secrets of wrapping. With three yards of fabric, she envelopes her body as if draping a column. She ties a little knot at the top, turns the fabric down like a narrow cuff and accents this simplicity with extra-special accessories.

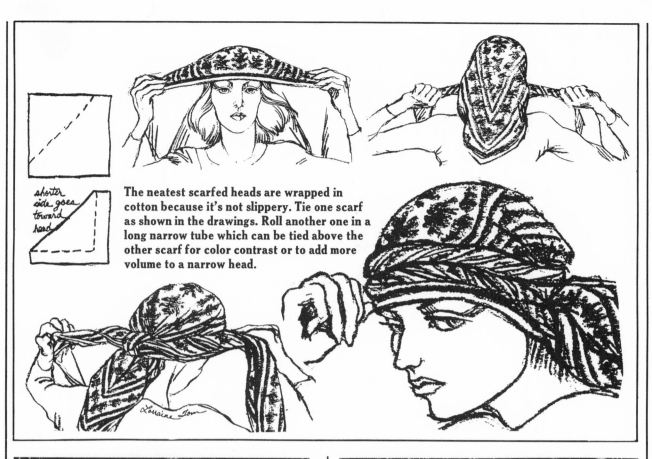

The neatest scarfed heads are wrapped in cotton because it's not slippery. Tie one scarf as shown in the drawings. Roll another one in a long narrow tube which can be tied above the other scarf for color contrast or to add more volume to a narrow head.

shorter side goes toward head

Acetate or silky jersey lends itself best to elegant wrapping. A skirt is a twist of the fabric and a tuck at the hip. Or use long yardage and invent variations on the same theme: Slip one end between the legs, shaping a halter top and strapless pantaloons.

Once in a while you may find yourself near water, wanting to swim but lacking a bathing suit. It's wonderful to go naked, but most places are still uptight about nudity outside the bathtub. With wrapping, you can always roll up your dress, pull the back through your legs, tucking the gathered fabric in the belt. Now you're ready to hit the waves!

around the waist or hips, the extra fabric is folded on top of itself in an accordion pleat at the front, then the material around the waist is folded over on itself to hold the skirt in place.

Rayon or nylon fabric is another inexpensive fabric to experiment with. You can cut yourself a sari length and still have lots left when you buy an $11 nylon georgette sari from an Indian import shop.

If you're uncertain with your knotting and tucking, add some insurance—a belt, tight at the waist, a brooch, or a big solid pin. In Bali they don't use buttons—the standard Balinese blouse is just held together in front with two or three safety pins. Most of the people use standard safety pins; the wealthier have more elegant models based on the same theme. You can put a security safety pin at the waist, the shoulder, or the center of the bosom and emerge with the cheapest chic on the beach!

Although it's quite difficult to get around a big city in wrapped clothes, you can still play with fabrics and patterns by wrapping lengths of cloth around your head. In the winter, nothing feels better than a nice tight head-wrapping. During the day, you can use bobbypins to set your hair in tiny pincurls and wrap it tight with a babushka. At night you may emerge with a superfluffy head.

One long scarf looks great knotted at the back of the head with the ends hanging down. Two Russian peasant flowered wool challis scarves look exotic wrapped and twisted over each other so that the patterns and colors contrast. Several scarves look fantastic folded and tied in the middle as a ponytail at the back of a scarfed head. That way you can have your "hair" and set it too.

Don't just stick to your neighborhood Singer Sewing Center. Polyester double-knits won't do. Try to track down the pure cotton and silks that make the best fabrics for wrapping. The range of silks carried at a little cubbyhole of a shop in Los Angeles called Oriental Silks is breathtaking. This listing hints at the wondrous variations of

The Halter

Another multi-purpose piece of cloth to own is this long rectangle of fine cotton or chiffon. For an instant top, put the scarf around your neck, pulling the ends out equally at arms length in front. Cross one over the other to tie in back. Depending on the length of the piece, you may even be able to bring the ends back around to tie in front.

fabric that still exist in the world: silk pongee, Poa Shan pongee, chefoo pongee, ya kiang pongee, pure silk chiffon so light it floats, China silk, Honan silk, spun silk for lingerie, Soo Chow brocade, silk satin, raw silk shantung, palace silk brocade, silk crepe brocade, Kuan Lo Siok crepe brocade, printed silk crepe, printed twill from Shanghai, silk satin tapestry, tinsel-mixed silk satin (said to be the most exquisite silk exported from the mainland), silk marquisette, silk brocade matting, crepe de Chine, Habotai silk, nubbly white silk, silk gauffer, and Po Po silk crepe.

162

Wrapped in white fox mixed with yards of tulle, Edita Sherman knows how to make that "grand entrance" and liven any party!

ZANDRA RHODES

Pushing Fabric to Extremes

Zandra Rhodes is an English designer whose chic is not cheap to her customers. But to her, and to anyone willing to work and push their imaginations to the utmost, the results can't be anything but individual and rewarding, whether one is designing clothes or just getting dressed for the day.

Zandra has been doodling, snipping, cutting, dyeing, sewing, pleating, and feathering clothes for almost a decade. Yet, today they sell in the hundreds of dollars, but she started with nothing other than her imagination, perseverance, and a totally fresh approach to what can be done with fabrics. Each new Zandra Rhodes collection becomes more personal, startling, and refined. Zandra's clothes are unlike anything you have ever seen or imagined. Solarized lilies, luminous pinks, ripples of silk jersey, an octopus of chiffon, yard upon yard of squiggled labyrinths unfurling to the tune of a mad samba, and now the grand elegance of minuscule pleats on long burgundy silk, and lace-entwined pastel chiffons.

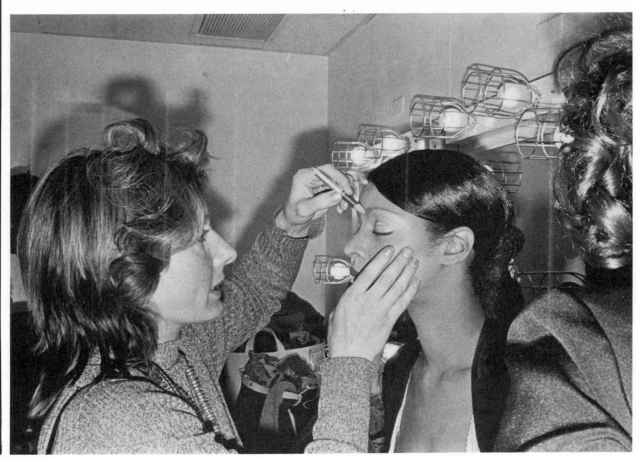

Far from trying to lead the same life as her moneyed customers, Zandra can often be found slaving away in her overcrowded London workroom wearing patched jeans and a silk jersey top over a black turtleneck, or driving around the States in a sleep-in van.

"I come from a very middle-class family near Dover, you know, sort of your average person. Well, I suppose my mother was rather extraordinary; she worked as a fitter in Paris for the couture house of Worth. She met my father, a truck driver, at one of those typically English ballroom dancing contest evenings. She would wear incredible multilayered bright tulle dancing dresses.

"Later, my mother taught at the college where I studied, so I never learned pattern cutting and practical sewing because that was the class she taught! Instead I studied textile design and went on to the Royal College of Art in London, where Mary Quant and a lot of people with new ideas were studying. That was in the pre-Carnaby Street days of London, and when I started taking my textile designs around to be executed, manufacturers kept saying, 'We can never sell these.' So I set up my own print workshop with a friend. And then when boutiques started springing up everywhere, I opened one with another girl, but we fought like crazy because she didn't like my designs. So I thought I better try my luck in America.

"I had to take a crash course in pattern making and then learn how to fit on a stand. I had no idea what the grain in fabric does. I made some terrible mistakes, but at least I had no preconceptions of how a dress was constructed. It was so lovely for that reason . . . bodices falling all over the place! I'm still learning, and it's only been a few years since I've actually sewn pieces of fabric together.

"Now when I show the collections, I stage a spectacular. For the first one I wanted a great Brazilian carnival feeling, mixed with a masked ball. The people who wear my dresses want to stand out in a crowd, not look quiet and secret.

"The more I try to analyze the kind of clothes I make, the more I find they stand on their own without precedent. People are buying an original—it's what I see that particular year. Those funny dresses I made one year with holes cut in them might not have sold very well when I did them, but

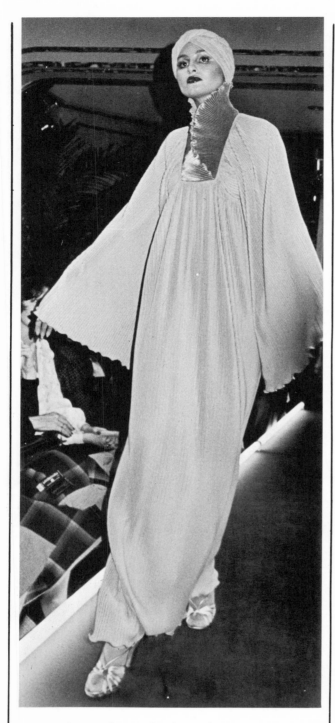

me. My partners used to say, 'For money's sake, Zandra, tone yourself down. You are frightening the buyers away!' But I don't do my makeup to spook people. It just feels fine to me to have fun with colors on my face.

"As long as you are prepared to make mistakes and have other people laugh at you, you can wear and create what you please. I have worn weird things and six months later looked at photographs of myself and thought, 'Oh God, how could I ever have looked like that!' There was one phase where I wore my hair pulled back and painted my face red on the sides. When I look back, it looked terrible, but somehow it was right for me because it pleased me first. I like to pursue ideas that amuse and surprise me, even if they are considered cheap and vulgar by most standards.

"A lot of people I know don't have any money and yet they look very special. It often has to do with the fact that you cannot define the value of what they are wearing, so their personality comes through. Tie a little chiffon handkerchief around your ankle and then wear something completely plain, or add a colored cord for a ring. Why be so status conscious with designer letters all over the place? It's sheer waste. There are plenty of good things everywhere. My bag, which I bought at a London department store five years ago, has gone through everything with me. So what's the point of spending a lot of money on owning a small 'status bag' if I have to carry three paper shopping bags around with it?

"I have to work extra hard because I am always going along my own way. It's not easy; I don't find the act of designing easy at all. I have to shut myself away to do it, even though I like people around. The actual creating part is hell, but the glossy part is easy. When you've done the clothes and you see people galloping around in them, then you're inspired. And you can get back to the locking-yourself-in-the-studio bit. Sometimes I am terrified! My mind becomes a total blank. Actually, I am glad when that happens, because when you get stuck you have to rethink and relook. Then I move along and don't fool myself with the same old ideas."

somewhere along the line they are going to make their mark. I believe my dresses never date. People will wear them ten years from now because I am not involved in trends.

"As far as my own way of getting dressed and made up is concerned, I feel totally immune to what anyone says. That's probably why I sometimes go around with green hair, red cheeks, and iridescent blue dots here and there. It's not that I have a fear of being anonymous. It's something else that drives

Some of Zandra's sketches from her earlier days, above and left, and a 1977 sketch, right . . . all fantasy!

WORK CLOTHES

The easiest style for working women is quiet uniformity punctuated with a special personal touch. If we're disillusioned with the high cost of uptown basics, we can track down lovely, inexpensive army-surplus and work clothes. Work clothes were built to fill a need. Since they were never designed to be in fashion, they can never go out of style. And though they are intermittently taken up as fads, whenever a manufacturer tries to knock them off, the imitation comes out looking silly and inept.

Some of the work clothes' colors are a drawback—who wants to look like the school janitor? But if the colors don't match your mood, you can dye them or punctuate them here and there with bright accents. While rejecting fashion, you needn't reject a look of individual charm.

SURPLUS PARADISE

The army-surplus store is the place to head for cheap status. "One might think that status and recession don't marry too well," wrote Enid Nemy in *The New York Times*, "and one might be wrong. The recession is here, but it hasn't driven away status—it's merely reversed it. It's no longer how much one has paid for something, it's how little."

In a time when it's almost impossible to afford top-quality construction, stitching, and fabric, you can find it surplus for low prices. For the person with a tight budget and an aversion to thrift shops, army-surplus stores are a cheap way to dress. The armed services, unlike department stores, do not take delivery on goods that do not meet the strict specifications of their contracts. The stitching is close and tight, the seams are often bound, and buttonholes don't unravel.

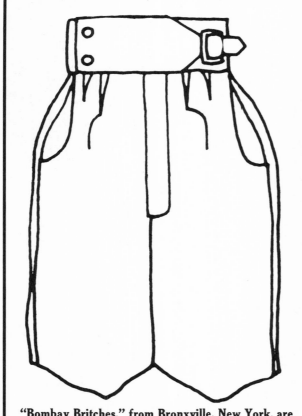

"Bombay Britches," from Bronxville, New York, are typical of classic English army-surplus gear.

In a world of synthetic blends and plastic ultrasuede, military clothes are almost the last inexpensive sources of pure cottons, wools, and leathers. And they last *forever*. Army-surplus means never having to say you're sorry.

For those who are still entranced by new silhouettes, perhaps the freshest look is short boots and the bloused pant, dropping to mid-calf or around the ankle, pants a bit big, pulled in at the waist with a knotted belt. This "look" can be seen in Israeli training camps and on the drill fields of Fort Hood, Texas, as well as in fashionable world capitals. It is ironic that a new silhouette is evolving from the regimentation of the military. If you play with these clothes you can develop an individual look. Khaki needn't belong exclusively to the military, just as red isn't the exclusive province of firemen. A regulation army raincoat becomes a nice background when you add a brilliant purple scarf or a fluffy fox collar. The dash of color and the softness of the fur destroy the military character the coat once had.

People were understandably reluctant to go to Vietnam in the sixties, but it seems now that everyone on the street has zipped into the **army field jacket.** For under $10, it's about the cheapest covering around. It's not rainproof, and it isn't too useful without the system designed by the army to go with it—the liner and hood. The field jacket is the hardest popular military design to wear in an individual way. But it does have mystique for some, perhaps it carries the romance of the invisible urban guerrilla.

Fatigues are made of green khaki and once functioned as the army's great equalizer. Within the service an elaborate status system evolved around this basically drab uniform. (Fidel Castro, after all, elevated fatigues to the status of black tie for formal occasions of state.) All military uniforms in America are designed at the U.S. Army's Natick Labs outside Boston. They are meant to work in an ordered system, possible when recruits wear only what they are issued, exactly as issued. But of course, no matter how functional the fatigues were, a soldier had to tighten up on the basic theme, embroider it, embolden it, upset the army's

Making work clothes work for you: black jumpsuit with angled zippers; bright red webbed belt with a brass buckle; knitted watch cap angled on the brow; red snap-closed nylon windbreaker. (And bright red lips and nails !)

Above: in sunny Southern California, where the body reigns supreme, they take their T-shirts tight . . . this one's with a surplus web belt and army pants dyed red, and comes from Camp Beverly Hills, where all those film types get the surplus-look together without trekking to the army-navy store (aviator glasses . . . very important.)

Left: an army-surplus beige cotton shirt spiffed up with a beautiful old belt and necklace from the Middle East.

order—for his personal dignity if nothing else. When recruits cut down and tailored their fatigues for that tight, sexy fit, the Natick "life support system" was shot to hell. The system was based on layering, but there was no way these soldiers could squeeze their winter sweaters and socks under tight fatigues. Luckily, we're not in the army and don't have to go on winter maneuvers or listen to the rules from Natick, so we can get our fatigues in any size, dye them any color, wear them loose or tight, or even chop off the sleeves or legs . . . systems be damned!

The army **fatigue shirt** is like a shirt and jacket rolled into one, with nice big pockets over each breast and sturdy welt seams. You can wear it tight as a glove over a turtleneck, unbuttoned to a knotted waist over a tan, or as a summer jacket with the sleeves rolled up over a T-shirt and drawstring-waited cotton muslin skirt.

Fatigue pants are designed to be bloused over boots. The army rule is that trousers are not to hang above boot tops, a holdover from World War I leggings which protected against mustard gas on the battlefield.

The aviator's companion, a durable navy blue nylon, fur-collared blouson jacket, which comes with a detachable quilted lining is made all the more attractive by this pilot.

Natick came up with **jungle fatigues** for the war in Vietnam, with roomy, snap pockets on the thigh and bloused drawstring legs that tied mid-calf at the boot to intercept insects and bugs.

It's best to buy fatigues that are older, because the modern "new army" has done away with pure cottons. Starched fatigues used to be a point of pride in the sixties—"breaking starch" meant putting on a nice crisp pair of fashionably faded fatigues—but now the army is designing things for washing machines rather than breaking starch. Fatigues are now of wash-and-wear synthetic blends.

You'll find it's difficult to get both a tight fit in the crotch and enough length in the leg in almost any military uniform, so consider taking them to a seamstress. Tuck the short pants into high boots or under a pair of crazy socks. (Take a look at the chapter on sports clothes: hockey socks? Baseball gaiters? Soccer stripes, perhaps?)

Several schools of blousing developed in the army over the years, and you might as well know what they are.

1. The George Washington School. The pant's leg is folded around the ankle, wrapped with 3-M® masking tape to hold the fabric tight, and then inserted into the boot.

2. The Blousing Rubber School. The blousing rubber is a big green fabric-covered elastic band similar to a ponytail holder. The band is snapped around the ankle, the trouser leg is tucked up under the inside of the rubber band, and *voilá*, a simple blouse.

3. The Blousing Ring School. The one person in ten who seeks true perfection inserts a heavy metal blousing ring, about six inches in diameter, down the leg of the trousers before using the blousing rubbers. The weight of the metal ring gives the bottom of the blouse that perfect, rounded shape. In theory, the blousing ring refinement is rather like the tiny golden chains Coco Chanel placed in the lining of her suit jackets to make them hang perfectly.

4. The Tin Can School. A number-ten vegetable can with both ends cut out and

taped is slid down the pants leg to give a smooth, even, blouse above the boots, but tends to clank while walking. Some blousing experts prefer a *Time* or *Newsweek*-sized magazine slipped inside the pants to give a stiff look to the leg. A magazine is much quieter than a tin can, and you can read it if you get stuck in line!

Once you've mastered the arcane art of blousing, you might as well top it all off with an olive drab cotton cap. Don't go too all-out with fatigues, or men will turn from you with horrible memories of mosquito-spattered training at Parris Island. Tuck in a blue pack of Gauloise cigarettes in the waist, put a pumpkin-bright T-shirt under the top, tie on a long, multicolored silk jersey scarf, turn up the collar and sleeves,

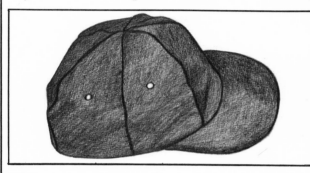

blouse the pants into your favorite boots, and you're Cheap Chic. The surplus outfit basics shouldn't cost more than $13–$15.

If you're one of those purists who search high and low for **pure wool socks,** we have it on good authority that the army issues the finest socks of the world's finest wool. Of course, they come in olive drab, but you can't have everything! At Brooks Brothers they would cost $5. Some surplus stores carry the British army sweater of thick-ribbed wool with canvas shoulder patches.

The **army-issue undershirt** is made of wool and cotton with a big crew neck and a long, long, knitted cuff on the sleeves. In a big size on a thin girl, it looks like a drop-shouldered beach dress, especially when tied up with a brass-buckled web belt or a classic silver antique or conch belt. Also nice in summer is the $1 khaki cotton undershirt. The quality is much better than comparably priced discount-store undershirts.

What a way to go to work—practical, loose and protected.

The big, mid-calf **army raincoat** is a fashionable alternative to getting wet. Over a sweater or two, it can function as a year-round raincoat. The designers of this coat weren't stingy: there is lots of room here for layering, because the cut is really ample. Not bad for $6.

A pilot's one-piece **flight suit** looks like a dashing coverall, with a zipped front and two diagonally cut zip pockets on the chest, and pockets here and there for maps and things. They come in brown or olive, cotton

Elaine Grove, illustrator and a star of the popular daytime soap opera, "Love of Life," in her off hours: she's wrapped a little boy's Western-style belt around the waist of used Walls Master Made coveralls from Texas, and she's peering at us through army-issue style tinted glasses, popular with everyone from McGeorge Bundy to Mick Jagger to Elaine Grove!

or wool, and at $15–$20 could be a year-round uniform over a silk shirt or turtleneck, or under a leather vest. (But remember that the jumpsuit and coveralls were designed for men. Like the leotard, it can be difficult to unlayer yourself when you have to run to the bathroom.) If you grow inordinately fond of the airman look, sink some money into a weathered leather flight jacket lined and collared with fluffy wool shearling. This jacket develops a rich and romantic patina with age and proper care.

For a more conservative effect, look for the below-the-knees classic blue wool **air force officer's overcoat.** They really knew how to make these right, and if you set a tailor to work on it, you can wear this coat from Wall Street to Walden Pond with ease. In quality and design, the officers coat is equal to a made-to-measure overcoat.

The dark blue **navy pea coat** is another almost-luxurious military classic, beauti-

Pants that take forever to unbutton but last and last.

fully designed in quality wool. Yves St. Laurent copied it almost line for line in his couture collection a few years ago and is returning to it again. You can get the original design for much less at your local army-navy store.

The navy blue **thirteen-button wool sailor pants** with black lacings can take you

A navy captain's coat is fine protection against winter wind.

through many winters, but beware of length because they are often too short to wear with heels.

The U. S. Navy also makes the very best **100 percent wool sweater** in a flat dark-blue knit that will keep you toasty warm and good looking. The navy sweater comes with long or three-quarter length sleeves for under $10. To keep your head warm, pull an inexpensive knitted navy watch cap down over your ears. (Your hair gets brittle, and over half your body heat can be lost by an uncovered head in the bitter cold, so cover it! Ears too.)

Navy surplus is also a rich source for perfect pale blue cotton **workshirts.** Sak's, Bloomingdale's, I. Magnin's, and Macy's all

WORK CLOTHES

American work clothes have been around in one form or another since the country was built, working on the railroad, down in the coal mines, busting sod, putting up skyscrapers, and digging subways. Their functional style evolved from a long line of anonymous designers and the demands of hard work. They've got integrity, stamina, good looks, and oh you kid!

Coveralls are worn by mechanics, freaks, artists, and just plain folks. Antonio Lopez, one of the most original fashion illustrators of New York and Paris, wears $20 khaki coveralls every day: "They're so comfortable and made so well that I live in them!" It is intriguing to think that Antonio—who

This is a cape made out of a flare parachute, with white British gurkha shorts, and suede and canvas ballet slippers (imported from China by Bowman Trading). The rest of the surplus comes via Camp Beverly Hills, where cheap is definitely chic.

sell dippy imitations in polyester-and-cotton blends, but the navy makes the real McCoy. Starched and pressed and teamed up with a fine silk tie, some men wear them daily to the office to give a tongue-in-cheek note to the suit-and-tie tradition.

More high style that can sometimes be discovered at army-surplus stores: Beige twill **shorts** with buttoned cartridge pockets and epaulets; khaki cotton pleated **walking shorts;** the classic **safari jacket** with epaulets, breast and hip pockets, back pleat and belt. The safari jacket is another military classic that has made its way from the streets to the couture houses of Paris. It's $80 at Abercrombie & Fitch, under $15 at a surplus store. Take a look in First Layers (Chapter I) to see how one woman uses the safari jacket as the year-round top-layer in a flexible clothing system. The U. S. Army Natick clothing labs would be ever so proud.

Carol Troy's outfit cost $9: $1 for the Boy Scout pants, $1 for the matching khaki shirt, $7 for a T-shirt with the Cheap Chic logo color-Xeroxed on the front. (And then there are the boots . You can bring them in at under $100.)

The French waiter's jacket ($12) from La Samaritaine in Paris, is available in similar styles at uniform supply houses in the States. Take a look at how well it works as a jacket (dressed up by grandmother's lace handkerchief in the pocket) by comparing it to a real waiter wearing it as a uniform on page 182.

discovers and styles some of the most beautiful and eccentric fashion models in the world—is fond of going around town in the lowly coverall.

Can't Bust 'Em brand coveralls have a multitude of pockets and are meant to withstand grease and grime and heavy washing, so a little city dirt doesn't faze them. Sweet Orr overalls in brown hard-hat style make you feel like a construction worker, with their bib front and suspender back. In gray pinstripes, they make you want to ride the rails; in denim you can tame the West or wrassle a commune to its knees.

What's blue, denim, and very baggy? **Carpenters' pants,** with a fascinating array of pockets down the side and mysterious loops and fasteners for hammers, chisels, rules, and flat pencils. Find them in white and dye them any shade you like. **Painters' pants** are another cheap, stylish way to dress.

Checked wool **lumberjack shirts** from

army-surplus stores are a handsome, sturdy classic, and the more expensive Pendleton soft wool plaid shirts are a worthwhile investment. Wear one under a riding jacket with a butterfly bow tie.

European work clothes offer all the good design and construction of the American breed, and give you that extra ripple of pleasure from finding something cheap, stylish, and really unique that no one has yet. Looking for work clothes is one way to see more of what a country's all about. A

Janitor's wear, the beige twill shirt, gets all dolled up.

friend of ours brought back a pair of pinstriped gray overalls from Prague just after the Russians had occupied Czechoslovakia. The saleswoman couldn't understand a country where rich students preferred wearing work clothes, and our friend couldn't understand why the Czechs didn't see the inherent beauty of a well-designed pair of overalls. It was an international standoff, but the Czech overalls were a big hit back in Boston.

La Samaritaine, the biggest department store in Paris, has several floors full of some very unexpected, beautiful work clothes. Their oatmeal linen **jewelers' smock** makes a very chic dress, with ample fabric gathered from an overstitched neckband and loose, gusseted sleeves. La Samaritaine also carries well-tailored overalls, black coal-man's suits, ciré fishmongers' tops, nuns' aprons, painters' smocks, dress-length sculptors' smocks, blue cotton electricians' jackets, butchers' smocks, and medical uniforms; all unchanged for a hundred years.

181

La Blouse des Halles is another Paris work-clothes headquarters. Here you can find bright orange polyester zip-up coveralls, a butchers' jacket in a small hound's-tooth check, the white garçon de café waiters' jacket in prices ranging from $15 to $20. The long doctors' coats are cool and crisp for summer, and cheap at $13; or you can fashion your own white "linen" suit by getting a $9 medical jacket to wear with sailor pants and a bright scarf.

The shop Sotovol in Paris caters to race-car drivers and aviators. The special Numero Uno **jumpsuit** opens with dual zippers from neck to leg, so you can put it on over everything you're wearing. This design has a stand-up officer's collar, chest and hip pockets, and two map pockets on the side of the leg. All this intricacy costs $50. It comes ready to wear or made to measure in poplin or gabardine of slate blue, mouse gray, chestnut brown, taupe, beige, or white. Or choose the parachutist's camouflage piebald coverall for $32.

There is also an extremely stylish shop in Paris called Globe, so severe it looks like a

Cheap protection against the rain is a simple beret along with a basic private's raincoat found at the surplus stores.

Take this white cotton jacket out of context, and you have comfortable, chic summer wear.

locker room. The owner sees work clothes as the only logical way to dress after the thirties-to-sixties revivals with all their kitsch overtones. In the midst of these riotous shapes and colors, Globe leans toward a sober chic which can look rather somber. If you wish to pass quiet and unnoticed, Globe will outfit you with work clothes imported from all over the world: French, English, and American army/navy uniforms from around the world, Chinese padded jackets, and Japanese street-workers' pants

A uniform, dyed a favorite color, could be a favorite dress.

and kimonos. "You say khaki looks sad," says the owner, Gerard Decoster, "but is shocking pink as gay as all that? I've been wearing khaki for six years now, and I've had a ball every day. And besides, for the quality of cut, stitch, and fabric, you can't find a better bargain."

PROFESSIONAL UNIFORMS

A Japanese painter lives in New York, buys medical uniforms, dyes them, and sells them to expensive department stores. She uses a particularly Japanese palette which ranges from dusky roses to deep violets that take beautifully on white cottons. Her most popular uniforms are the short surgical gowns and long wraparound patients' gowns with loose raglan sleeves and little ties in the front, short wraparound operating jackets, button-front cotton short-sleeved nurses' uniforms, and three-quarter-length duck lab coats. Other specialties are hand-dyed 50¢ cotton petticoats with eyelet-trimmed

By gosh, Osgood never tires of his Osh-Kosh.

hems found on Fourteenth Street and sold for summers at the beach with an undershirt of a similar shade.

Hotel and restaurant supply houses carry perfect white waiters' jackets, kitchen pants, and big wraparound aprons to color for summer covering and winter jumper

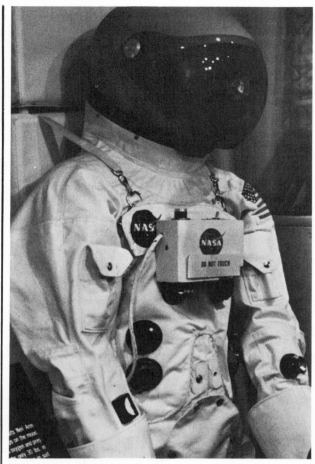

The most perfect and advanced of all jumpsuits or work clothes is also the most useless garment for earth-wear!

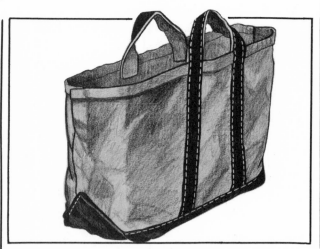

The canvas tote for shopping, week-ending, or whatever.

wear. You can find large **canvas totes** at supply houses such as the All-Steel Scale Company in New York. They sell mail totes and leather-trimmed canvas bank-note bags that you can have monogramed and made to order in the size you like for $30 to $50.

If you're looking for an inexpensive yet classic blazer, track down the department store that carries uniforms for the most exclusive girls' or boys' school in town. One friend of ours in San Francisco bought a single-breasted navy wool school blazer which was actually the uniform for Miss Burke's School, added special English buttons, had it shaped by a seamstress, and has been wearing it on and off since 1962. It now needs only a new lining—not bad for $30. While you're in the uniform department, see if you can dig up a crisp little nanny's dress, a school's cotton shirtwaist, or sturdy brown walking shoes. School clothes are rather appealing once you're not forced to wear them. The best places to find

used school blazers are the exchanges run by the private schools to raise money for charity and scholarships. The Spence-Chapin Exchange in New York occasionally has uniforms on its racks, and once in a while an absolutely breathtaking couture debutante gown will make an appearance.

If you have a little girl, ask friends going to France to buy the adorable little button-front, long-sleeved school uniform called a "tablier," which can be found in most hosiery or haberdashery shops for $1. The older the store, the bigger the chance of finding an old stock of these pure cotton uniforms.

Wendy frolicks in her "le tablier" school-girl dress.

BETSEY JOHNSON:

Fanciful Young American Design

Dear friends — I'M HAPPY TO HAVE THE CHANCE TO WRITE TO YOU.......to LET YOU KNOW HOW MUCH I APPRECIATE YOUR INTEREST IN MY WORK. I ESPECIALLY ENJOY HEAR-ING FROM SOME OF YOU...FRIENDLY LITTLE LETTERS, LETTING ME KNOW THAT YOU'VE MADE UP ONE OF MY PATTERNS † YOU LIKE IT A LOT....MAKES ME FEEL VERY GOOD. ...KEEPS ME GOING. SO I THOUGHT I'D LIKE YOU TO KNOW ME BETTER.

Betsey Johnson sizzled onto the fashion scene in 1965 as top designer for Paraphernalia, where she kept churning out unique styles—the skinny T-shirt dress, tiny undershirt tops, miniskirted A-lines—pop clothes that were a jumping reflection of those heady days of the "youth revolution." Betsey was our own homegrown Mary Quant, a designer of immense talent and energy. She went on to Puritan, Alvin Duskin, Alley Cat, Capezio, I. Miller Shoes, and during the "baby years" (Lulu was born in '75) "free-lanced all over the place, but basically I went back and forth to Hong Kong for a junior manufacturer. Now she's got her line, "Betsey Johnson," "very sexy, modern, graphic, 'look at me,' almost like Paraphernalia come full circle, but my taste and my lines are just more grown-up. It took me eight

SUN + MOON IN LEO...TAURUS RISING.

MAYBE CHILDREN'S PATTERNS... NEXT: TOY CLOTHES!

ME. AUGUST 10, 1942. WETHERSFIELD, CONN. THE ONLY THING I KNEW WAS THAT NOBODY COULD GET ME OUT OF MY HAND-ME-DOWN LITTLE RED WOOL DRESS..WITH REAL PEARL BUTTONS!? MAYBE MA MADE IT. WHEN I HAVE KIDS I'M GOING TO MAKE THEM EVERYTHING THEY PUT ON.

months. Nobody wanted to take the risk of backing me. 'We don't know what the new direction is,' they'd say, and I'd say, 'I AM the new direction! Why wait!'' She continues her involvement with Betsey, Bunky, and Nini, a New York boutique that serves as a laboratory of ideas for top designer Betsey Johnson.

"All my work is really a good time. I approach it thinking 'would I want to wear it?' But I don't want the manufacturers to think the way that I look is the way my work looks. I want to get them to think of my work as separate. So I wear my housedresses or old jerseys up to their offices. After leaving Alley Cat I realized that I had this terrible freaky Junior Designer image, and it's hard negotiating with businessmen who are trying to play dumb and pretend that they think you can't design anything else. But these stupid jobs become challenges! It's a challenge to use cut chenilles and mohairs and the colors I want. Despite the problems, I love mass-market and inexpensive stretchy stuff. I like to work in an isolated way—a private clientele would involve a lot of socializing.

"My ideas come from everywhere—I guess you'd say I'm eclectic. I get ideas from the costumes I used to make for dancing school as a kid; from those T-shirty kinds of baby clothes. I go to the textile library at the Metropolitan Museum—but if they see you doing anything more than looking, they rush out with big sheets of plastic to protect the fabric! And I visit the Philadelphia Museum, which has a great collection of old American work clothes. In terms of countries, I get most ideas from South America, India, and Turkey. I used to make fabrics and clothes out of India, Turkey, and Hong Kong. And colors—in Burma, those saffron-robed monks in the middle of all those shades of green—that registers later, when you're designing.

"I'm so tactile that when I teach for free I blindfold the kids so they can really feel things. I think that the tactile sense is the most important thing to have in your work, being able to feel how something is going to fit on your body.

"My ideal would be to sell one item a week on a corner, Saturday afternoons. The people would know I'd be on the corner with pants one week, then matching tops the next . . . that way I could do what I wanted in any colors that I wanted, and they wouldn't be marked up. I know women I'd love to have here in my loft just sewing, sewing. If you keep it to one style a week a lady can make it quite fast. Of course, you'd have to guess at the fit. You couldn't try my things on, just like Biba T-shirts. But I think the person I sell things to has a sense of holding things up to her body and seeing if they fit. I never try things on when I shop. But that's my dream—a street-corner operation—because I never have an outlet to do exactly what I want. I know I'm more proud of the T-shirts and pants and drawstring skirts than of all the expensive, overdone things at Betsey, Bunky, and Nini, where I know the prices are too high but don't have any control!"

MAYBE CHILDREN'S PATTERNS... NEXT: TOY CLOTHES! YBE

OH... I REALLY WANTED TO BE A DANCER..... MY GREAT TEACHER WOULD LET ME DESIGN ALL MY SOLO COSTUMES. MY MOTHER MADE THEM. I STILL HAVE EVERY ONE. I'D MAKE DOLL CLOTHES OUT OF THE VERY UNUSUAL FABRICS, SEQUINS, CHINA SILK, TARLETAN, LAMÉ + GLITTERED NETTING.

TOO BAD... NOTHING AS FANTASTIC AS PARAPHERNALIA COULD LAST.

+ HERE'S ME IN A TV STUDIO IN NEW YORK... THE ALL TIME "CITY OF MY DREAMS" AFTER GETTING AN ART DEGREE, WINNING MLLE. G.E. CONTEST... WORKING AT MLLE MAG... GOT A JOB AT THE MOST FANTASTIC "DESIGN WORKSHOP" (1965)..... I COULD ALWAYS SEW + MAKE MY OWN PATTERNS... + FOR 3 YEARS MADE ANYTHING I WANTED TO.... I LIVED IN SILVER TAP SHOES, TEENY TINY SKIRTS + REALLY STARTED DOING MY BODY-BASIC T-SHIRT STUFF.

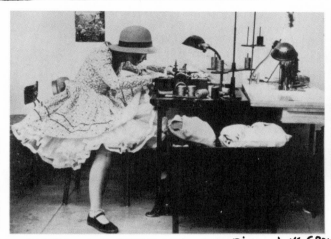

DEBORAH TURBEVILLE

W.W. DAILY

INDIA WHERE I LIKE TO GO MOST.

SO...HAPPILY ON TO "ALLEY CAT" + BUTTERICK...A.C.'S GROWING UP...BUT BUTTERICK IS GETTING MORE + MORE FUN. LOTS OF "CRAFTY" STUFF...LIKE THE IRON-ON DRAWINGS "APRON-KIT"...I LOVE TO MAKE THINGS THAT. NO MANUFACTURER COULD TURN OUT IN MASS-PRODUCTION. VERY PERSONAL...CREATIVE THINGS. MADE WITH CARE + PRIDE.

OH DEAR....MY "BRAD-OFF THE BOAT PERIOD"- (JUST OVER.) I'M A LITTLE SWEDISH + LIKE TO WEAR PEASANT CLOTHES BEST. THE EARLY 70'S-I WAS DOING MY "OWN THING" NOT WANTING TO LOOK LIKE ANYONE OR ANYTHING?

FOR BUTTERICK I'M GOING TO STICK WITH "CRAFT" THINGS----

D.T.

I LOVE THESE PICTURES BY DEBORAH TURBEVILLE.

GODFREY...I LOVE CLUTTER! HERE'S MY WORKROOM...I LIKE CLOTHES TO LOOK LIKE THIS. VERY PERSONAL, LOTS TO LOOK AT. EVERYTHING'S AN IDEA OR SOMETHING THAT AMUSES ME...OR JUNK.

I THINK ITS BEST TO SAY HERE....THAT YOU CAN DO ANYTHING YOU REALLY WANT TO....THERE'S NO "SECRET" WAY. JUST LOVE + DESIRE....I THINK....+ AS A FRIEND JUST TOLD ME...REMEMBER....YOU CAN NEVER HAVE TOO MUCH FUN......

MY LOVELY SEC. LYDIA...VACATIONING.

AND BARBARA WALZ.

D.T.

+ YES...MY DEAR WORKROOM "LADIES" THAT MAKE MY DAYS PEACEFUL + HAPPY. WE'VE ALL BEEN TO-GETHER FOR YEARS. CHELENA, EMMA, MAGDA + CHERRY ALL WORKING TOGETHER...OUR FAMILY. APART FROM THE "RAG" BUSINESS.

+ TODAY....HENNA IN MY HAIR...STILL BASICALLY IN T-SHIRTS + FUNNY BOTTOMS. I'M MOVING INTO A BIG LOFT DOWNTOWN + FEEL LIKE I'M STARTING FRESH. THAT FEELS GOOD. XOXO LOVE, BETSEY.

LUCIAN K. TRUSCOTT IV

Playing the Market

Lucian K. Truscott IV is a journalist and author of The Complete Van Book and the novel Dress Gray. He is a graduate of West Point, where four years in the cadet uniform taught him to appreciate the freedom of expression clothes give the individual. He now lives in New York and is at work on his second novel. "I wear my old army T-shirts when I write," he says. "I guess I still equate sweat with work, so those T-shirts are the bottom line of my wardrobe.

"When I was seventeen I worked in a men's specialty shop in Alexandria, Virginia. Those were the days of Bass Weejuns and Gant shirts, and rebellion was defined by the boldness of your madras plaid. That year I learned about clothes. I watched ties widen from 2⅜ inches to 2⅝ inches, lapels creep toward the shoulder seam of your sport coat. I spent a year watching the men's clothing marketplace at work. I discovered this: they work on you, and if you want to be

different, you've got to play the market.

"This is how it shakes down. Levi's were hip for about a year, then the marketplace absorbed them and turned the cultish arrogance of jeans into a garment version of fast food. It's happened to every break-away style that's come along since. Right now, it's almost impossible to achieve sixties-style individuality with clothes.

"Me? I just keep playing the market. If you can't stay one step ahead in style, then beat them on price. I buy everything I own at ½-off list, nearly wholesale. I pick up 'out-of-style' suits and sport coats and shoes and salt them away for a couple of years and wait for the market to circle around; then I jump on, pull out the old stuff, and ride the curve. After inflation and the dollar jack-up of the 'latest style,' you end up saving about 75 percent by simply biding your time. Things move so fast these days, everyone forgets you can play the market at your speed."

The 50 percent solution: Lucian's jacket was half-price from Alan's Apparel in Albuquerque, designed by Ralph Lauren for Chaps. His Jaeger 100 percent cotton shirt with a striped body and white collar? Also half-price. The pants, by Yves St. Laurent for Men, one-third off at Bonwit Teller. And the shoes? From the Gucci factory, and sold off-season at half-price for $35 at Shep Miller's in Southampton. The car? $700.

THE MIXES

Once you have set up your basic uniform, a few special classics, and some thrift-shop finds, how do you go about putting them together for the way you live, be it in Portland, Oregon; Albuquerque, New Mexico, or Buffalo, New York? This chapter will show you the different ways people put themselves together. They can be quite extreme, but we think you will find hints, ideas, and inspirations from all of them. We want you to see the kinds of individual styles that never make it to the fashion magazines. Ultimately, the crux of Cheap Chic is learning to put things together for the person you imagine yourself to be. Some of you may want exotic evening fantasies; others may go for a sexy but ladylike elegance; and others, just that special accessory that lifts the basics out of the uniform category and gives you an individual stamp. The way you put things together tells others and yourself that you care about feeling good, which is, after all, the point.

LINGERIE

Those night-sparkled seamed stockings give us a hint as to what lingerie has become in recent years, more an accessory than a necessity. It wasn't until the early seventies that the full range of underwear stopped selling: the half-slips, full-slips, panties, bras, girdles, or garter belts with thigh-high stockings.

A sexy, feminine, classic design by Fernando Sanchez.

Once these items went out of favor, brains started to percolate, and stylish girls realized that these once-utilitarian items can be put to the nonutilitarian uses of enticement, seduction, and humor. Seamed stockings with a garter belt are downright sexy, especially with a pair of marabou-trimmed satin mules. You can even pull off the effect of seamed stockings when wearing pantyhose. Biba makes seamed pantyhose in a mind-boggling array of colors for under $1 a pair. If a friend goes to London, ask her to buy some for you in the one-size-fits-all.

Tight panties and bikinis can be rotated with silky, open-leg, lace-trimmed shorts, like the ones worn in the twenties. These floppy pants allow the body to breathe, and look surprisingly sexy, both naive and knowing. Fernando Sanchez designs the sensuous underwear that shows up in the fashion magazines and is being copied by all the manufacturers, but thrift shops still hide the most luscious pure-silk styles. Even if your underpinnings never show, you get a charge of erotic energy just knowing you're wearing the most beautiful, silkiest lingerie imaginable under your plain T-shirt and jeans. Or, on the other hand, you may get the same effect knowing you are wearing the tackiest, hardest sex-queen lingerie ordered directly from the catalog master himself, Mr. Frederick of Hollywood.

Janet Reger's filmy concoctions from Beauchamp Place, London: all silk and all heaven.

Antonio's antic sketch of legs, legs, legs, chock full of ideas you can adapt to your life. Look across these pages: here are ballet-slipper type soled flats with tights and legwarmers, men's argyle socks you might wear under slacks, flat, comfy Mary Jane's with anklets under long, baggy slacks.

LOTS OF LEGS!

Leg dressing is one game you can really play on a low budget. You don't get too many tips from fashion magazines, because, after all, how much do socks cost! But they can give you more bang for your buck . . . from textured pantyhose to shocking-pink legwarmers . . . than almost any other element in your wardrobe. And this is especially true if you keep your wardrobe pruned to one or two basic colors.

Jacque McCord, an editor at *Modern Bride*, says they're doing all sorts of things with legs all of a sudden. They're shooting pictures of brides in midcalf or ankle-length dresses, for instance, wearing ivory point d'esprit or textured stockings so their legs look more delicate.

Modern Bride, she says, has a whole closetful of ribbons. "They're from Hendler's, *the* ribbon store in the garment center, on West Thirty-eighth Street. So you can decorate your ankle with a ribbon, maybe with a flower knotted on it, like an ankle bracelet. You can even thread sneakers or any lace-ups with long ribbons, then tie them up around your ankle over a pair of ankle socks to get that fat blousy look with pants—say, midcalf—or a tight-wrapped look with pegged pants." She also suggests that pants in a light fabric might be pegged tight, to make a new shape out of old, at the dry cleaner's or tailor's. These look great with very high heels.

Jacque herself wears men's socks under her boots in the winter. First, she says, you don't run your nylons unnecessarily. Second, you get good insulation, especially with cotton socks. She feels men's socks come in both a better quality and range than those available now for women. And she often wears mules, both summer and winter, because her shoes get a lot of wear and tear. Once these leather slip-ons begin to stretch, she starts wearing them with her

Soft ballet slippers with a satin bow at the throat, elastic across the arch, and feminine little white anklets . . . for the young at heart! Midcalf cowboy boots with men's work socks; and flats worn under a petticoat with the stockings rolled down around the ankles, fifties style.

favorite men's (or women's) socks, as both a color accent and to keep the shoes on her feet!

Polly Mellen, the fashion editor of *Vogue*, is known for putting together beautifully patterned and textured outfits in neutral tones and then sparking them with a flash of color at the ankle . . . like peach-pink angora socks with a pair of really good heeled moccasins (and *everything else* beige). There are incredibly wild things to be done with socks; but subtle touches like this are the unexpected glints that really pull an outfit together and give it flair.

Ki Hackney Hribar, who covered the top American designers for *Women's Wear Daily*, is now editor of the new Sunday-supplement *Style Magazine*. She's a self-confessed conservative dresser but still has lots to say on the subject of legs.

"I wear socks to rejuvenate my old shoes," says Ki. "Good, expensive Gucci-style moccasins with heels—I usually buy mine at Shoe Biz or Charles Jourdan—al-

ways seem to *stretch*. But you can get the heels and soles fixed, keep them nice and polished, and keep them your size with socks. Then you can still wear them weekends with pants." Ki also prefers men's socks, because they are often higher, but finds women's manufacturers are starting to make good socks now too. "Men have interesting argyles," she says, "plus 'preppy' colors like red, yellow, lime-green . . . with all-black or all-navy clothes I like the psychological lift of bright-colored socks. Last summer I got bright red socks from the boy's department of a store in Southampton. Conservative men's stores are always dependable places to shop . . . for women! Now, I might even wear subdued argyles to work if I'm wearing all black. Or even a pair of pink or metallic turquoise socks!

"When you're wearing jeans, play around with your legs. It's fabulous to have these colors and patterns sticking out. It's a relatively inexpensive way of having fun . . . and I'm basically *conservative*. I always

Granny's high-heeled lace-ups with baggy legwarmers; high-heeled backless springolator stilettos with wrapped ankles, and ankle-fastened boots with slim pants tucked into them . All ideas . . . all rather stunning!

keep a supply of black and brown knee-highs on hand to wear with pants. But you need a little color sometimes. What's fun is to wear neutrals and then play around with your legs because it's so cheap!

"For the office," continues Ki, "I always keep a stock of black, brown, and sometimes gray and burgundy opaque pantyhose on hand. They can even be a bit sheer if they show good color. Buy one pair to check on their size and opacity, then six at a time for black and brown, three at a time for your two other basic colors.

"Recently, I've started to fool around with the opaque striped and textured pantyhose for the office and I love them! I always like it, even with a tweed. There's nothing wrong with a patterned leg." Ki also wears the textured legs when there's something going on in her shoe, like perforations or a two-tone leather like a spectator pump. "A lot of women might be nervous about wear-ing patterned hosiery with anything but a simple moccasin," she says, "but you shouldn't be afraid to go ahead and wear textured hosiery . . . it looks good!

"Bendel's in New York carried the point d'esprit pantyhose for the winter of 1977. It was so chic in black! By this winter, hopefully, all the stores should be carrying them." The big, inexpensive department stores like Mays in New York are *good* resources, she finds. They keep stride with fashion and are now carrying textured and patterned pantyhose. They needn't cost a lot of money: Keep an eye open at the volume stores, the bargain basements. Ki's burgundy striped pantyhose were $1.59 at Mays. And it's certainly more fun to play with a cheap striped leg than sticking to the basic $1.39 nude sandalfoot. You certainly don't have to pay $4 or $5 to get fashion diamond-patterned pantyhose—you can get something similar for $1.59!

Antonio's favorite slim leg and high, high heels again, next to flat, crushy soft leather boots with a bright shot of legwarmers over them . . . comfy and warm for the winter, but only for the very coldest days.

In the evening, Ki wears men's gangster-style striped silk or rayon socks in black. The problem? They're often too short. And in the summer, when it's hot, what can you do but get a tan and go without stockings to the office, or play around with textured sheers. And it's always good to have a supply of knee-highs in nude to wear under slacks if your shoes are uncomfortable without socks.

If you're going to go without stockings in the summer, Ki recommends leg waxing for some women. "It's such a relief, it's like a tranquilizer! You just don't have to worry; it's worth every single penny. Depending on how many years you've been doing it, you can go about every three weeks in the summer and every six to eight in the winter." Elizabeth Arden salons around the country are supposed to be excellent, if this proves to be your summer treat.

And of course there are toenails . . . paint them some color you'd *never* consider wearing on your fingernails, like firehouse red, burgundy, mauve, metallic anything! Check out the dime store for the loudest colors you can find.

What about the fashion of wearing short cotton anklets? They look great on Gilda Radner on "Saturday Night Live" (she decorates them herself with little rhinestones and stuff), but Ki Hackney doesn't think they're really *her!* "I'm 5'10½", so the idea of me putting all that height on little white anklets doesn't appeal to me! But you do have to be more willing to experiment. We just did a Ralph Lauren fashion shooting for *Style*, and he sent over these blond woolly knee-socks for the model to wear with a bare, suede high-heeled sandal underneath a simple, classic cashmere sweater dress. It *sounded* so bizarre to me, but it looked terrific when the model put it on!"

THE BARGAIN HUNTER

Sophie uses her face as the strongest, most extreme aspect of her appearance. She will never go out in public without having her face done in the palest foundation, her eyes heavily outlined in a smoky gray, and her mouth painted a dark, shiny plum. On other days it will be other colors. Accentuating her strong face will be another strong color, the rich henna shade rinsed into her thick hair. Sophie is known in Paris as one of the most extravagantly dressed women around. Whatever she wears is an original Sophie concoction. She always looks extraordinary on very little money, with a lot of imagination, experimentation, and practice. By trade, she designs textiles and sportswear, and when she's not at the office she's home, compulsively decorating and redecorating her apartment.

Sophie's secret is a willingness to push a look as far as it will go, trusting her eye to find the prize yardage hidden in a stack of mediocre fabrics on sale at the big department stores; trusting her luck to dig up the perfect bits of fur to transform simple cloth into rich exotic gowns, and knit caps into romantic Russian fur clouds floating above her brow.

She always tries to buy everything wholesale, telling manufacturers she's in the trade and hoping they'll sympathize. You can try this in New York or other large garment manufacturing cities on the weekends, or find a friend who has an in with a manufacturer. Clothes are usually half-price, if not less, when bought wholesale.

Sophie makes a masterful use of bits of **fur trim,** adaptable to almost any climate. For instance, in Los Angeles, where it is seldom bone-chillingly cold, a designer cuts striped Mexican serapes into bright, long, conch-belted coats, hangs raccoon tails

198 | **The secret shopper: Sofi puts together the most extravagant creations from bits and pieces of sale goods in Paris.**

Simple and elegant: plaid on the bias, hanging in large triangles, topped by a babuska and strong makeup.

tremes—use it to further your fantasies rather than just to keep you warm. So she plunked down all her money on a royal blue fox neckpiece on sale at a top furrier instead of opting for a sensible used fur coat from the Ritz Thrift Shop. No one ever forgets those crazy blue foxes nuzzling her neck, and somehow she manages to keep warm. Exaggeration is its own reward.

Larissa Jarzombeck is another New York City fur freak. After coming to New York from Europe, she said, "I had to cope with the overheated apartments and freezing streets. The logical solution was to dress lightly in silk chiffon and wear fur close to

The contrast of fur against day clothes: a bowtie bristles against a warm, puffy old raccoon coat.

along the sleeves and the yoked cowboy-style back, then fluffs a fox collar around the neck. There are all sorts of ideas here for transforming a thrift-shop find into a deluxe western look.

The contrast of fur with extreme combinations of fabric and patterns is really arresting, like fur on a soft-flecked wool jersey lined with a check-tablecloth plaid. A seamstress in Paris called Galiana makes odd use of fur by draping the skin of the animal around the front of a coat and down the sleeve, wherever it lands, then stitching it in place. It looks as if some pelt fell out of the sky and just happened to land on the coat. The very primitive treatment of the fur on the tailored wool coat is an odd sight.

One young fashion editor in New York feels you should always take fur to ex-

the body. Nothing like that was available, so I bought some lamb skins in the fur district and put them together like a jigsaw puzzle. The result was so shocking that for two weeks I dared only to wear it at night!

The first day I ventured into the sunlight, I ran into Miles Davis, who ordered a white one, and later many more. This started a word-of-mouth clientele, mostly musicians and artists." Larissa's coats are sensible, durable, and handsome. Like the royal blue foxes, they are not cheap.

STREETWISE

Marcia approaches a stylized look from the other direction. Instead of furs and luxuries, everything she wears is from a thrift shop, but layered flippantly and combined with ethnic favorites in a really in-

Marcia's street chic mixes well-worn thrift shop buys, exotica from abroad, and unexpected layers, then adds a scarf at the neck to tie it all together.

genious way. Everything she wears is tiny, tiny, tiny. She'll wear a miniskirt, for instance, but
• Sling a belted Peruvian bag around the waist, and
• Add silver-trimmed hand-tooled cowboy boots.
To get a couple of lengths going, she'll wear

Colette livens up a discreet beige outfit with Indian silk.

a mid-calf coat with a tiny waist over the short skirt, and tie a shiny yellow 59¢ Woolworth's scarf in a practiced knot at her neck. Marcia is not trying to tell people she is a lady of luxury; she's telling them she's an independent soul with enough imagination to pull the most disparate bits and pieces into a very personal look. This streetwise look says she's an artist of the first order.

If you study photographs of people who have a finely tuned sense of style, almost invariably you find a **scarf.** Knotted at the neck, draped over a coat, twisted around the head, tied at the waist—scarves show up everywhere. Since fashion magazines often have to show some rather uninspiring dresses manufactured by their major advertisers, they have developed the skill of transforming the ordinary into the exceptional through the use of scarves, belts, and other accessories. Nearly every page of *Vogue* is a lesson in the uses of scarves.

Start up a collection of scarves from thrift shops or Woolworth's and add the cheap cotton squares sold in summer. Try to get different sizes in your favorite colors. Experiment until you feel ready to sink some money into a crepe de Chine square for head wrapping, a silk muffler for the neck, or whatever it is that will give you the most pleasure. The same goes for **belts**—they can change the look of almost any outfit. Try to get as many inexpensive belts as you can find: wide cinch belts in your favorite colors, narrow leather bands that can be worn singly or three at a time, plus an investment belt or two (see Chapter II, Classics).

Perching a **hat** atop your head every morning is a sure way of creating an image. We're not talking about wearing a lot of hats that are in, like a stiff new gaucho hat tied under the chin. We're talking about hats that look better and better as they become more and more you. Some people grow so attached to their hats and their hats to them that they become virtually inseparable; look at Congresswoman Bella Abzug. One of the most original and talented stylists in New York is never seen without his

Hats can create and extend an image...in John Wayne's case, it's rough, tough, and very, very tall.

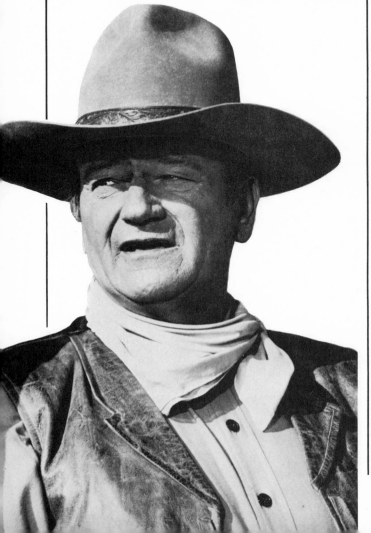

Make a hat your own by adding a personal touch.

trademark Japanese student cap festooned crown-to-brim with the charms of a decade of friends and travels. He is always dressed in black. All his decorative impulses go into his work and into that extraordinary, glittering, charm-laden cap.

CONSERVATIVE MIX

Andrea Quinn, a beauty editor at *Seventeen*, is another person seldom seen without a hat, a man's battered old felt hat with a slouched-down brim. Andrea is as selective and consistent about the other clothes she wears as she is about her hat. She wears a very toned-down mix of the classics, work clothes, cowboy things, and thrift-shop finds. She prefers old, well-worn clothes to the mania of seasonal fashions she sees covering the market in the showrooms of Seventh Avenue. Her apartment on New York's East Side is a reflection of her understated style: pared down, almost severe, with classic American quilts and bare wooden floors.

Andrea's basic working uniform is jeans and gym T-shirts with two shifts of jewelry, either ethnic things in silver, or gold antiques and family hand-me-downs. "I don't like new clothes very much," she says. "I used to O. D. on fashion all the time. When I was first a fashion editor, I got a lot of stuff because I could get it half price. But it gets to be too much. Now, if I'm expected to look like a fashion editor then I do, but most of the week I wear very simple things." These are the things that get the most wear in Andrea's closet: Frye boots, St. Laurent boots, cowboy boots, a $6 army-surplus raincoat, an old riding jacket, T-shirts and jeans, a French jeweler's smock, thick sweaters to pile on under the unlined raincoat in the winter, and a collection of old patterned vests she slips on over everything. "It's really weird," says Andrea. "I'm a fashion editor, but I just don't dress myself up much anymore. I've found I like wearing very simple things."

Dalila wears her best fur jacket with second-string classics, gold jewelry, a Cartier watch, and a tight pair of recycled Lee jeans.

Conservative Mix: To one oatmeal linen dress, Andrea adds worn St. Laurent boots, an antique knit vest, beat-up riding jacket and a battered hat from a flea market.

Holly's sensuous jerseys: the dirndyl pants are a day and night constant. Here, a silk crepe de Chine head-wrap, antique fur, and her dyed jersey bandeau.

NAUGHTY BUT NICE

Holly Harp has probably never worn a Mr. Frederick's original, but she doesn't have to. Her designs have been described by customers as "naughty but nice," just the kind of thing for the sexy, body-conscious, but upstanding ladies of Los Angeles. Clothes that bear her label are expensive, but Holly's style doesn't have to cost a lot. It's a system of simple, sometimes whimsical, clothes centered around her basic silk jersey dirndl pants and, quite often, her exercise leotard. The mix will take her from her factory to exercise class to a party in the Hollywood Hills. Because of the free and open way people dress in southern California, Holly never worries about looking overdressed. She just wears what pleases her.

The Holly touches that enliven her basics are:

These pants are Holly's "jeans." Here she wears them with an old belt, capelet, and Lycra exercise leotard.

• A scalloped capelet that was a *Ladies' Home Journal* home sewing project in the forties, decorated with mysterious drippings she has not been able to re-create.
• A piece of chiffon made into a belt for the twenties diamenté belt buckle she found at a thrift shop.
• A silk crepe de Chine scarf wrapped around her head, peasant-style.

All her colors are in a muted range of smoky violets, grays, and greens, so everything mixes with everything else. The strong, simple impact of Holly's style leaves little room for showy jewels or accessories. Cheap Chic comes in knowing when to subtract from a look as well as when to add to it.

ECLECTIC ELEGANCE

Françoise Kirkland is a lady whose clothes energies go into tops and shoes. Her look is totally eclectic, with an international ring to it. She grew up in Paris and eloped with an American. That was ten years ago, and Françoise still shows that kind of headlong daring in her life and style. Having recently moved from New York to the Hollywood Hills, she is studying journalism at UCLA and developing a new set of thrift-shop contacts.

A typical Eclectic Elegant outfit might combine a bit of everything: wrapping, sports, thrift shops, classics, ethnic, work clothes, basics. Pegged jeans from France with that special tight cut, well-worn suede boots, a $2 Hawaiian print shirt from a rag house bundle, an Isotonic Lycra leotard, and traveler's jewelry: a single earring made from a child's silver bracelet hung with feathers, beads and bits of leather; a silver-studded bracelet from New Delhi; bangles from Morocco; a Cartier tank watch with a

Francoise sports the look of an Angeleno Mixer. Her heavy wool coat is made by Barbara Hokonson of New York's Copper and Decay.

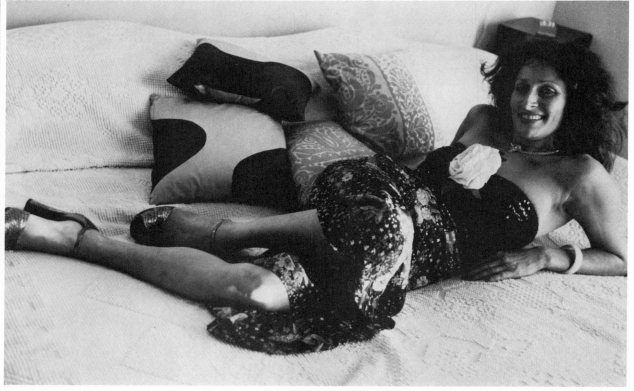

Jazzy day-into-night clothes, left, by Norma Kamali. The suit teams up with anything from drawstring pants to a ruffled evening skirt or all-out Chinese robe glamour. Francoise, above, wears her go-everywhere top.

brown leather band; a bolo tie from Arizona; and a gold chain hung with *figas*, charms from friends, and a childhood St. Christopher's medal.

All this stuff piled up on one person could court disaster, but Françoise puts it together with a practiced eye and a sense of humor:
• The jeans are rolled up over the boots.
• The Hawaiian shirt is knotted in front over the leotard like a calypso dancer's,
• and all the heavy jewelry just seems to fall into place, perhaps because it's all of such quality.

Tune into Soul Train when you're running low on ideas!

Short, short-shorts, georgeous Tibetan boots (available by mail order), over-the-knee socks: that's imagination.

And Françoise loves wraps. "I make a turban out of this huge piece of tie-dye you just wrap and wrap, whatever way you can manage to keep it on your head! You can also wear it as a sarong skirt. One night I went to Claridge's in London in knickers with the scarf wrapped around my head. The headwaiter said I wasn't allowed in the dining room because I wasn't wearing a skirt. So off I went to the ladies room, took the scarf off my head, and wrapped it into a skirt. They had to let me in!"

Women between eighteen and thirty-five are said to spend over $10 billion on clothes each year. Some of the women in this chapter spend a bit more, and some make a point of spending much less than average. But whichever camp they fall in, they get ten times the mileage and ten times the fun out of their clothes because they've developed their unique talents for making chic from cheap.

A directory of stores, flea markets and mail order houses in the U.S., England and France.

Our listings could never be all-inclusive, and regrettably we have missed many excellent stores. Also regrettably some of the store listed may no longer be in existence as you read this. The purpose of the listings was to give you an idea of what to look for. With this in mind we suggest the following:

Check your local phone book for the address in your town of Goodwill, Salvation Army, Volunteers of America, Catholic Charities, and charitable thrift shops.

Check your newspapers for church, school, and charity rummage sales, flea markets, yard sales, and the like.

Don't overlook the Five and Ten in your town. Woolworth's, McCrory's, and other large chain variety stores offer a wealth of Cheap Chic.

United States and Canada

ARIZONA

How Sweet It Was
636 North 4th Ave.
Tucson
Vintage clothes, an assortment of original designs, and recycled denims.

Phoenix Art Museum Shop
1625 North Central Ave.
Phoenix
Ethnic folk patterns.

ARKANSAS

The Left Bank
One McIlroy Plaza
Fayetteville

Lois Gean's
109 South Jackson
Magnolia

CALIFORNIA

LOS ANGELES AND
SOUTHERN CALIFORNIA

Aardvark's Odd Ark
Los Angeles
(3 locations)
Tremendous selection of used clothes, generally under $10.00.

Anne's-tiques
Main St.
Santa Monica
Antiques at excellent prices.

Bazaar de Mundo
2754 Calhoun St.
San Diego

Bun-Ka Do
340 East First St.
Los Angeles
Amazing selection of Oriental trinkets.

Camp Beverly Hills
9640 Santa Monica Blvd.
Beverly Hills
International surplus antiques and creative used clothing. Army-navy gone chic.

Copeland's Enterprises, Inc.
233 Madonna Rd.
San Luis Obispo

Dasu-suda
614 North Doheny Dr.
Los Angeles
A sassy boutique.

Eclectiquaria
8939 Santa Monica
Hollywood

Eric & Company
6915 Melrose Ave.
West Hollywood

Fiorucci
Los Angeles
Italian design shop with American panache.

The Flying Emery Board
Beverly Hills
A real investment for fingernails.

Harold's Place
420 North Bedford
Beverly Hills
Classy antiques.

Headquarters Army-Navy Store
131 East 6th St.
Los Angeles
A local favorite.

Holly's Harp
Sunset Blvd.
West Hollywood
Sexy, ladylike clothes.

Julian's
3716 Sunset Blvd.
Silverlake, Los Angeles
Underground ethnic, gorgeous Chinese jewelry.

Junk Store
Wilshire Blvd.
West Hollywood
Good used clothing.

Kobo
1446 Camino Del Mar
Del Mar

Lame Deer Indian Store
8009 Santa Monica Blvd.
Los Angeles
Western apparel.

Los Angeles Museum of Art
Museum Shop
5905 Wilshire Blvd.
Los Angeles

Los Angeles Uniform Exchange
5239 Melrose
Los Angeles

Manchee
334 First St.
Los Angeles
From lovely, tie-dyed double
comforters to geta sandals on stilts.

Maxfield Bleu
9091 Santa Monica Blvd. and
Doheny
Los Angeles
Terrific European imports, expen-
sive but choice stuff.

Mehitabel
3716 Sunset Blvd.
Silverlake
Scarves and cottons from India,
exotic beads and amulets—all at
reasonable prices.

Miss Amber
Los Angeles
6640 Hollywood Blvd. Hollywood
Beverly Hills too.
Flash and dazzle; first with English
scarf dresses.

Ola Hudson
Melrose
West Hollywood
The funky forties feel, custom
designed.

The Orient
6626 Hollywood Blvd.
Hollywood
Real finds; cotton and silk kimonos
hidden among the standard tourist
items.

Oriental Arts
325 First St.
Los Angeles
Antique Orientalia in brass,
bronze, and cloisonne.

Oriental Silk Company
8365 Beverly Blvd.
Los Angeles
Beautiful silk fabrics, robes,
scarves, crocheted tops.
Send for catalog.

Pasadena Flea Market
The Rose Bowl
Pasadena
The biggest.

Pierre La Jond & Co.
516 San Ysidro Rd.
Santa Barbara

Pillars of Eagle Rock
Eagle Rock (near East L.A.)
The Loehman's of the West—
designer clothes at less than half
price.

Pleeze
708 North Curson Ave.
West Hollywood
Antiques.

Post Exchange
18433 Plummer St.
Northridge
Surplus.

Rainbow Resource Co.
1048 Hermosa Ave.
Hermosa Beach

The Red Balloon Ltd.
168-63 Algonquin St.
Huntington Harbor

Repeat Performance
7621 Melrose
Hollywood
Antique clothing.

Right Bank Clothing Co.
Beverly Hills
Now has snazziest shoes, too.

The Supply Sargeant
631 Santa Monica Blvd.
Santa Monica

Surplus Marts
6263 Santa Monica Blvd.
(corner of Vine)
Los Angeles
Army-navy surplus.

The Surprise Store
Los Angeles
Like New York's Unique Clothing
Warehouse—in Culver City and
other locations, too.

3 Plus One
219 Manhattan Beach Blvd.
Manhattan Beach

Topanga Threads
110 North Topanga Canyon Blvd.
Topanga
Macy's and the big stores find
things here.

The Trunk Salon
8701 Santa Monica
West Hollywood
Antique clothing.

Vanity
704 North La Cienga Blvd.
Los Angeles
Franklyn Welsh's beauty
emporium.

Wylan Gallery
9619 Brighton Way
Beverly Hills

Zaca
Los Angeles
Carries Lily Bleu—fabulous shoes.

NORTHERN CALIFORNIA

Abbe's
1420 Clement St.
San Francisco
Antique and secondhand clothes.
Most look new and barely worn.

Bary
125 Geary
San Francisco
Stylish boutique.

Bizaare Bazaare
5634 College Ave.
Oakland
Lots of antique finds in clothing,
hats, jewelry, feathers.

Carousel Resale Shop
1642A Irving St.
San Francisco
Used clothing with sensational
buys from the thirties.

Casey's Faded World
2265 Upper Market
San Francisco
Embroidered kimonos and satin
acetate lingerie.

Chicken Little's Emporium
1108 Polk St.
San Francisco
Crazy gifts and clothing; great
shoes and accessories as well.

Coastside Corral
Oddstad Blvd.
Pacifica
Full line of Western gear.

Cottonworks
137 Forest Ave.
Mill Valley

County Fox
10821 North Wolfe Rd.
Cupertino

Dark Horse Trading Co.
Mill Valley

Divina
60 Maiden Lane
San Francisco
To eyeball Fernando Sanchez,
Ralph Lauren, Dorothee Bis, New
Man Jeans.

East-West Leathers
Sausalito
Also at Grant Street in San
Francisco.
Leathers that last.

Far and Few
1510 Walnut Sq.
Berkeley
Quality antique clothing at fair
prices.

French's Hitching Post
1205 Third St.
San Rafael
Shop for Western wear.

Good Measure Fabrics
322 Miller Ave.
Mill Valley

Green's Boot & Saddle Shop
12153 San Pablo Ave.
Richmond
Another "don't miss" for Western.

Janan Resale Fashions
1432 California
San Francisco
Buys on secondhand designer
clothes and shoes.

Kaplan's Surplus & Sporting Goods
1055 Market (near 7th)
San Francisco
Check for army-navy surplus and
utilitarian looks.

Lost Horizons
2003 Fillmore
San Francisco
Up-to-the minute styles, cheap to
expensive, in a fantasy setting.

Lucette
77 Bridgeway
Sausalito
Original things no one else has.

Macy's
Union Square Shop
San Francisco
Go to the shop—fantastic.

Miki
Ghirardelli Sq.
San Francisco
(also on Telegraph in Berkeley)
Select boutique.

Ming Quong
1517½ North Main St.
Walnut Creek
Ethnic, handmade clothing,
jewelry. This store has quite a
history. It was named after an
orphanage and means "Radiant
Light."

Nasi
1156 Taylor
San Francisco

Next-To-New Shop
2226 Fillmore St.
San Francisco
Operated by the Junior League—
terrific for classics.

New Ideal
1336 Grand
San Francisco
Clothing for men and women, all
organized by racks. No fitting
rooms; good buys.

New York Fabrics
245 Tamal Vista Blvd.
Corte Madera

Obiko
3924 Sacramento
San Francisco
Expensive, unusual jewelry; unique
designer clothes; satin shoes from
Hong Kong.

Oui Oui
1529 Shattuck
Berkeley
Children's shop—everything from
French flea market to hand-dyed
Oshkosh overalls.

The Outdoorsman
197 North Main St.
Bishop

Painted Lady
Divisadero
San Francisco
Antiques.

The Palace Museum
1546 Polk St.
San Francisco
Elegant funk, specializing in
recycled clothing made from old
jeans.

Panache
Sacramento St.
San Francisco
Nice taste for a limited budget.

Pauli's
Broadway
San Francisco
Nice old clothes.

Poppy Fabric & Trim
1845 Solano Ave.
Berkeley

Pretty Mamma Inc.
1012 Pacific Ave.
Santa Cruz

Robert Kirk, Ltd.
150 Post St.
San Francisco
Tops in men's classics. Send for
catalog.

Ron Richards Saddlery
2510 Telegraph Ave.
Oakland
Wide selection of Western wear.

Satin Moon
14 Clement St.
San Francisco
Wide variety of fabrics: cottons,
silks, wool, Dutch wax, Liberty
House prints, crepe de chine,
gabardines, old buttons.

Second Hand Rose
3326 23rd St.
San Francisco
Fantastic emporium where you can
find racks of antique and period
clothes.

The Street Shop
4100 19th St.
San Francisco
Best for used men's wear—lots of
quality at bargain prices.

Tail of the Yak
2632 Ashby
Berkeley
Even more Oriental than San
Francisco's Thousand Flowers.

Thousand Flowers
311 Grant St.
San Francisco
Unusual, fantastic clothing and
gifts from all over the world.

COLORADO

The Deb Shop
123 West 4th St.
Pueblo

Denver Army Store
Denver
Here's the place to shop in Denver.

La Boca Ltd.
2412 East 23rd Ave.
Denver

La Piuma
Aspen

Last Tango
Boulder
Wonderful dress shop, stylish,
splashy.

The Lotus Eaters' Boutique
27 East Platt Ave.
Colorado Springs
Make most of their own things,
carry European garments, all
natural fibers and recycled drapery
fabrics.

Marcy's
203 South Galena St.
Aspen
Although geared more toward
women, tends to be fairly unisexual
with a range in style from fatigues
and plastic to silk. Prices range
from $1.50 to $350.00.

Uriah Heep's
P.O. Box 1362 Jerome Hotel
Aspen
Snazzy as the Jerome Bar! And you
can send for mail order too.

CONNECTICUT

Gorden's Bootery Inc.
936 Chapel St.
New Haven

Revival
213 Main St.
Westport

The Seraph
Good Speed Landing
East Haddam

DISTRICT OF COLUMBIA

Deja Vu Antiques & Objets d'Art
1675 Wisconsin Ave.
Georgetown
Vintage clothing 1900-1950s: hats,
purses, furs, fans, jewelry,
collectibles.

Sunny's Surplus
3342 M St., N.W.
Georgetown
Georgetown headquarters for
army-navy surplus. Sunny's first
gained fame in Baltimore,
Maryland, where they still have a
store.

Vernon's
1055 Thomas Jefferson St., N.W.

FLORIDA

Adam's Rib Boutique Inc.
Santa Rosa Mall
Mary Esther

Army-Navy Surplus
700 West Broward Blvd.
Ft. Lauderdale
Dash in for a khaki T-shirt to wear
as a hot-weather tank top.

Edge City
1017 Park St.
Jacksonville

Palm Beach Thrift Shop
Palm Beach
Beautiful tailoring, sumptuous
beading . . . the impeccable castoffs
of the luxury trade.

GEORGIA

Razzle Dazzle
2823 Peachtree Rd.
Atlanta

ILLINOIS

Ann Taylor
Michigan Ave.
Chicago

The Blue Parrot
217½ South 6th St.
Springfield
Buy, sell, trade men's and women's
old clothing, accessories.

Bottega Glaseia
49 East Oak
Chicago

Fiberworks
2364 North Lincoln Ave.
Chicago

Sami
3755 North Freemont St.
Chicago

Stanley Korshack
Michigan Ave.
Chicago
The Windy City's special specialty
store.

Steve Starr Studios
2654 North Clark St.
Chicago
Art deco, art moderne, jewelry,
furnishing and accessories.

Ultimo
114 Oak St.
The ultimate European boutique
look. The ultimate prices, too.

IDAHO

Boise Art Gallery Shop
Julia Davis Park
Boise

Yellow Brick Road
Ketchum

INDIANA

The Bootlegger Inc.
1016 Broadway
Fort Wayne

L. S. Ayres
Indianapolis
Look for Unique Clothing
Warehouse department.

IOWA

Crest Bootery/Coach 'N Four
104-106 North Maple
Creston

Things, Things, & Things
130 South Clinton St.
Iowa City

KANSAS

Collage Ltd.
1008 Main St.
Goodland

LOUISIANA

The Front Run
1305 Dublin St.
New Orleans

Jeans
2707 Williams Blvd.
Kenner

Rivet, Haute Coiffure Boutique
236 Metairie Rd.
Metairie
Hair, cosmetics, fashion.

MAINE

House of Logan
Booth Bay Harbor

MASSACHUSETTS

Armadillo of Boston
134 Newbury St.
Boston

Central War Surplus
433-435 Massachusetts Ave.
Boston
The place to look for army-navy
surplus finds.

Dorothy Dodd
57 Suffolk St.
Holyoke

Earthwares, Inc.
103 North Pleasant St.
Amherst

GB Ltd.
115 Newbury St.
Boston

Glad Rags
76 Church St.
Lenox
Fills 5 rooms on the ground floor of
a beautiful stained-glass-windowed
Victorian house. Stock: new
imported, domestic, and handmade
clothes. Also recycled and antique
"Little Rags," a kid's version.

Honey Suckle Rose
Winter St.
Edgartown
Fancy old women's clothing and
reproductions. Open summer only.

Song of the Road
Union St.
Vineyard Haven
Wearable folk art and handwork—
Central and South America.

Take It Easy Baby
Circuit Ave.
Oak Bluffs
Funky old clothing, mostly from
Europe. Open through December.

MICHIGAN

The Red Flannel Factory
Cedar Springs

MINNESOTA

Depth of Field
405 Cedar Ave.
Minneapolis

MISSISSIPPI

Dixie's
Starkville

Fashion Station
2131 24th Ave.
Meridian

MISSOURI

Famous–Barr
St. Louis
Look for Unique Clothing
Warehouse department at all 3
branches.

Macy's
Kansas City
Look at their junior clothes.

NEBRASKA

Hitching Post (men's)
Wooden Nickel (women's)
144 North 14th St. Lincoln
333 North 72nd St. Omaha
15 West 23rd St., Kearney
Specialty apparel and shoes. Fast
moving.

NEW JERSEY

The Cellar
Woodbridge Center
Men's and women's clothing.
Antique and new designs. Hand-
crafted clothing and jewelry.

Fly By Night
18 North Washington Ave.
Bergenfield
Items from over the rainbow and
around the universe. In a mall, but
customers are made to feel at
home. Imports and originals.

Island Shop-Man Stop
4205 Long Beach Blvd.
Brant Beach

The Last Straw
317 Glenwood Ave.
Bloomfield
Fine handcrafted jewelry,
distinctive clothing, gifts,
decorative accessories and
paraphernalia.

Little People Clothing Company
12 South Fullerton Ave.
Montclair
Fantasy in a brightly colored
gingerbread house over 100 years
old. Merchandise for children.
Handmade toys and imported
clothes, getting away from pink
and blue.

Marcia's Attic
213 Main St.
Fort Lee

NEW MEXICO

Alan's Apparel
57 Encantada Sq., N.E.
Albuquerque
Only store in 400-mile radius with
classic menswear—no doubleknits.

Gallery One
620 Sierra Dr., S.E.
Albuquerque

Kidstuff
230 Park Ave.
Raton

Wild Rose
2916 Central S.E.
Albuquerque

NEW YORK

NEW YORK CITY

ABC Antiques
122 Prince St.
Antiques, bargains.

Albert Hosiery Stores
Eight branches in Manhattan.
Full line of Danskin leotards and
tights.

Alexander's
731 Lexington Ave. (at 58th St.).
Department store with little-
known areas of designer copies and
inexpensive European imports: the
"Next Shop."

A. Altman
204 Fifth Ave.
French Imports, Calvin Klein,
Stanley Blacker; tailored suits.
Reduced prices.

Ann Taylor
15 East 57th St.
(also in D.C., Conn., Mass., N.J., R.I., Chicago)
Career-oriented clothes with great style that you can build on from season to season.

Arden's
1014 Sixth Ave. (near 38th St.)
Knit clothes, broad-brimmed velours in many colors, and broad-brimmed straw hats—all at low prices.

Artbag
735 Madison Ave.
Mail in your worn but classic bag for an estimate for repairs. They give a one-year guarantee on all work.

Atabex Boutique
243 East 53rd St.
Custom copies in wool, silk and silk/polyester blends—Calvin Klein, etc.

Azuma
415 Fifth Ave., and branches
Cotton scarves, straw hats, cotton skirts, blouses, dresses.

Bargains Unlimited Thrift
1429 Third Ave.
Guccis and Puccis alongside junk as low as 25¢.

Barney's
111 7th Ave.
Classics for men and now women. Special Italian and French designer imports.

Beckenstein Woolens
125 Orchard St.
Fine woolens, men's suits.

Henri Bendel
10 West 57th St.
Train your eye with the best of European and American ready-to-wear. Shoe Biz has the best, most stylish shoes in New York. The "Street of Shops" is a free amusement!

Bloomingdale's
Lexington & 59th St.; Bergen County, N.J.; Garden City, N.Y.; Short Hills, N.J.; Stamford, Conn.; White Plains, N.Y.; and D.C.
The hottest merchandisers with the hottest merchandise. Instant boutiques with runaway looks.

Bogie's Antique Furs
201 East 10th St.
Antique furs and clothes, with new bundles arriving twice weekly.

Bonwit Teller
721 Fifth Ave.
Someting special to train the eye in Missoni Boutique, Valentino's Piu, the Hermes shop and Turnbull & Asser menswear.

Bottega Veneta
655 Madison Ave.
Silk squares of crepe de chine from Milan; beautiful leather goods and bags for people who don't need designers' initials.

Brooks Brothers
346 Madison Ave. (at 44th St.) and branches
The store for American classics. Send for catalog and for the location of store near you.

Budget Uniform Center
110 East 59th St.
Lab coats, nursing, and waitress uniforms. Large selection of hospital "scrub" clothes for dyeing which can only be purchased by the dozen.

Buffalo Weavers Clothiers
203 East 60th St.
Smashing young Italian imports; great for ideas of what European trendies are wearing. Also Kensai imports from Japan. (Check this whole block of 60th Street: boutique paradise.)

Camouflage
141 8th Ave. (at 17th St.)
Men's classics and sportswear.

Camp & Trail
Park Place (near City Hall)
Clothes for the *Field and Stream* effect.

Center Thrift Shop
120 East 28th St.
Some things priced, some not. If you're in the neighborhood, it's worth a stop.

Charles Jourdan
700 Fifth Ave.
See it here first for the footsies.

Charleston Market
21 Second Ave.
A huge selection of thirties clothes.

Cherchez
864 Lexington Ave. (at 65th St.)
Beautiful Victorian camisoles, slips, dresses for summer; in perfect condition.

Chinese Emporium
154 West 57th St.
Utilitarian Chinese workers' jackets, other items from China.

Chipp
14 East 44th St.
Full line of traditional, English-oriented men's clothes.

Chocolate Soup
249 East 77th St.
Darling children's clothes; also, the mail-order Danish schoolbag that's a great carryall.

Chor Bazaar
801 Lexington Ave.
A wide selection of cotton, muslin, scarves, dresses.

Cora and Laura
369 Canal St.
Early antique clothes; Edwardian lights; silk stockings; doodads; pretty lacy stuff. A Wendy Whitelaw favorite.

Diamond's Secondhand Clothes
42 Hester St.
Every day but Saturday. Caters to men only. All suits are marked "fair," "good," or "excellent," and range from $1 to $30.

Dianne B.
729 Madison Ave.
Imports from France. Issey Miyake, Cygne, and Dorothee Bis designs. Very *Elle* magazine, very chic. Not very cheap.

Double Dealers, Ltd.
1364 Lexington Ave.
Children's resale store.

Dudley Eldridge
39 West 32nd St.
Custom-made shirts.

Early Halloween
180 Ninth Ave.
They carry a wide selection of old clothes, old shoes, and wonderful suspenders.

Echo Scarf Co.
485 Fifth Ave.
(682-5430)
Write or phone for store near you.

Eddris Shoes
314 East 78th St.
Secret source for the shoes for the yearly Madison Avenue boutiques co-op fashion show. Very reasonable original designs.

Emotional Outlet
91 7th Ave.
Young designer clothes at excellent prices ($8-$40).

Encore Resale Dress Shop
1132 Madison Ave. (at 84th St.)
Where the local upper-East-Siders take their year-old designer clothes.

Equator
79 Wooster St.
Antiques.

Everybody's Thrift Shop
324 East 59th St.
Some of the most well-heeled New Yorkers donate their clothes to the ten charities represented at this shop.

Farkas and Kovacs, Inc.
1187 Lexington Ave.
The most exquisite custom-made shoes for men and women.

Folio
888 Madison Ave.
All sorts of little books and notepapers. Beautiful Susan Suble calling cards made up with your choice of fifty designs.

Fiorucci
125 East 59th St.
American designs reinterpreted with Italian panache.

Fonda's
168 Lexington Ave.
Designer clothes (Marta Salvatore, Cacharel, Carol Horn, Cygne, Kenzo, etc.) and antique clothing at wholesale or discount prices.

Forty's Wink Antique
Fashion Boutique
1331A Third Ave.
Good assortment of antiques and children's clothes.

Freshwater Mfg. Inc.
716 Broadway (at 4th St.)
Used blue jeans, fatiques, sailor pants, army-navy overcoats. Old dresses, coats, scarves; and new T-shirts in a rainbow of colors.

Frugal Frog
1707 Second Ave. (near 88th St.)
Clean, very cheap. Thrift shop for children with amusements for the children while the mothers shop.

Gladstone Fabrics
16 West 56th St.
Carries many fabrics from the forties and fifties. They will match a color swatch for $7, no matter how much fabric you need.

Greenwich House Thrift Shop
273 Bleeker St.

Grizzly Furs
7 St. Marks Place
Military surplus, navy blue winter coats from England. Furs.

Gyro Surplus Corp.
Broadway & Bleeker St.
Large supply of work clothes.

Halina's Beauty Shop
160 West 55th St.
A seventh heaven of antique combs and hairpins...ivory, sterling, gold, amber, from the 1850's to the 30's.

Happiness Thrift Shop
1444 Third Ave.
Run for the benefit of the United Cerebral Palsy Associations of New York.

Harriet Love
412 West Broadway
Classic antiques from a lady who really knows her business.

Havona
110 Thompson St.
Contemporary and antique clothing.

Herbert Dancewear
1657 Broadway
Full line of Danskin dance supplies and Herbert Economy leotards, tights, and skirts.

Herman's
15 West 38th St.
Well-made hats at reasonable prices: velour, beaver, straw, or fabric from about $10 to $15. Ribbons, flowers, and feathers to choose for a personal touch.

Herman's Sporting Goods
42nd St. and Sixth Ave.
Sweat chic; top to bottom and back.

Hornblower Antiques
Canal St. & West Broadway
A good place for used clothing.

Hudson's
Third Ave. at 13th St.
Army surplus but often jammed, and grouchy salesmen. Brown leather motorcycle jackets and a large stock of jeans and work clothes.

Ina
105 Thompson St.
Soho shop, special lingerie, shoes, scarves, one-of-a-kind Soho artists.

Jackie Rogers for Men
27 East 67th St.
Men's clothing, many imports, excellent taste, rather expensive.

Jenny B. Goode
1194 Lexington Ave.
Mini department store. Inexpensive and unusual clothes and accessories with dash.

Jezebel
265 Columbus Ave.
Antique clothes in top condition. Good shopping area around this store.

Julie Artisan's Gallery
687 Madison Ave.
Art fashion from America's traditional craft techniques: weaving, knitting, painting, crocheting.

Julio's
867 Madison Ave.
One-size-fits-all concept in the most exquisite fabrics and exquisite prices...good for ideas.

Kamali
6 West 56th St.
Brilliant disco dressing, sexy draped jerseys and tight leggings. Norma Kamali is an endlessly inventive designer.

Kasoundra Kasoundra
(777-9851, by appointment)
One-of-a-kind, handmade, patchwork clothes of unusual fabrics. Crocheted Art Nouveau-ish handbags in antique frames.

Kaufman Surplus & Arms
Broadway & Houston St.
Jeans, army surplus, and work clothes.

Kaufman's
139 East 24th St.
They carry everything for the rider and Midnight Cowboy.

Kip's Bay Boy's Club Thrift Shop
1577 Third Ave.
Worth a stop as you tour the Third Avenue thrift shops.

Lady Madonna
793 Madison Ave.
The breakthrough merchandisers in stylish maternity dressing.

Larissa Designs
118 Forsyth St.
Fur coats, worn inside-out so the fur is next to your body. Phone first: 431-4295.

The Leader
305 West 125 St.
Army surplus and work clothes uptown.

Lee Ann Thrift Shop
215 East 59th St.
Handpicked, funky clothes & jewelry.

Le Gaspi
743 Madison Ave.
Jewelry by Richard Erker. From doing LaBelles costumes in the village, Larry's moved his fantasia uptown to Madison.

Le Grand Hotel-Tales of Hoffman
471 North Broadway
The classy Soho look defined—downtown elegance. Shoes, too.

Fred Leighton
763 Madison Ave.
The best deco, 40's and 50's jewelry in white, yellow, and pink gold.

Life Style Antiques
46 East 57th St.
Collectors of the very best antiques drop in here.

Loehman's
9 West Fordham Rd.
Bronx
The prototypical designer discount store—surely you've seen it in fifties movies. Take the IRT Lexington Avenue #4 to the Fordham Road Station. It's there on the corner of Jerome.

Lonia
55 W. 55th St.
Fashion forward, one-of-a-kind items, quality-conscious, natural fibers. Lots of personal attention.

Macy's at Herald Square
The world's largest store: if you can't get it here, it probably doesn't exist. Juniors on Four is like walking through *Cheap Chic*!

Mater's Market
237 East 53rd St.
Maternity shop.

Medusa
1207 1st Ave. (at 65th St.)
All kinds of adorable accessories: French and English hair combs, barrettes, bracelets, pins, necklaces, boxes, little purses, scarves, masks, at reasonable prices.

Memorial Sloan-Kettering Cancer Center Thrift Shop
1410 Third Ave.
The best to the worst: furs, clothes.

The Merchant of Venice
159 Prince St.
Italian clothing. Crazy!

Michael's Resale
1041 Madison Ave. (at 79th St.)
Great buys on designer clothes; all in excellent conditon.

Miller's
123 East 24th St.
Horsey-set central. Jeans, jodhpurs, riding boots, everything.

Miso Clothes Ltd.
416 West Broadway
Sparkly clothing—Cathy Hardwick, the young designers, very Soho chic.

M.J. Knoud
716 Madison Ave.
Ivy league, horsey shop: riding clothes, books.

Montenapoleone
789 Madison Ave.
Lingerie exclusively from Florence: silk nightgowns, hand embroidered silk delicacies.

Moroccan Fashion & Art, Ltd.
818 Third Ave.
Importers of Moroccan and Tunisian classics, such as solid black capes, cotton hooded jackets, leather gold-embossed slippers.

Mythology
370 Columbus Ave.
A shop of wonderful surprises behind the Museum of Natural History. Great for gifts!

The Nearly New Thrift Shop
54th St. at Ninth Ave.
A well-heeled group gives donations here, so keep trying.

Neighborhood Thrift Shop
449 Second Ave. (near 25th St.)
The last Monday of each month is sale day—half price for everything on the racks.

The New World Gift Shoppe
906 Madison Ave. (near 73rd St.)
and also at
1131 Amsterdam Ave. (near 116th St.)
Oriental garments, jewelry, and gifts.

Odyssey House Thrift Boutique
861 Third Avenue (near 52nd St.)
Shoes are the hottest item right now, both used and new. There are also a number of new clothes that sell for about 40 percent less than they would in typical boutiques.

Ohrbach's
5 West 34th St.
Department store with copies of designer clothes and inexpensive European imports, as well as masses of inexpensive merchandise.

O Mistress Mine
143 Seventh Ave. S.
New and old dresses, always changing. It's their policy to underprice.

Ophelie
673 Madison Ave.
Imported French jewelry; the tiny earrings make the store special.

Opportunity Shop
46 West 47th St.
Perhaps the largest thrift shop of all, with two selling floors, and four storage floors that add new items every day.

Opportunity Shop of Community Service Society
(oldest charity in New York)
46 West 47th St.
Quantities of nice stuff.

Palma
77 Wooster St.
Some Soho-designed antique and handmade clothing, plus antiques.

Paragon
17th St. and Broadway
Sporting source.

Paris Fashions
270 West 38th St. (17th fl.)
Designer fashions, wholesale prices, suits, separates, raincoats, blazers, capes, and more.

Pentimenti
126 Prince St.
Antique clothes, in Soho.

Planned Parenthood Thrift Shop
324 East 59th St.
Good variety of children's clothes.
Theatrical and antique clothes are
another feature.

Plymouth Shops
Fifth Ave. & 52nd St.
A good place to find inexpensive
accessories.

Propinquity
243 Third Ave. (near 20th St.)
Pretty antique costumes.

Resale Shop
802 Lexington Ave. (62nd St.)
High quality, low quantity,
pleasant help.

Richards Army-Navy Authentics
233 West 42nd St.
Army-surplus classics in an
exciting area.

Ridge Antique Furs
33 West 8th St.
(and the Warehouse at 55 Great
Jones St.)
For years a favorite of chic New
Yorkers with little money. Their
fur coats range in quality from
tattered to flawless.

Ritz Thrift Shop
107 West 57th St.
Use your old fur as a trade-in. If it's
in good condition, Ritz will fit,
process, clean, and glaze your
purchase free.

Runner's World
275 Seventh Ave. (near 26th St.)
Head to toe for sweat clothes.

S & W
165 West 26th St.
All designers, 1/3 to 1/2 off.

St. Laurent Rive Gauche Boutique
855 Madison Ave.
YSL's ready-to-wear shoes and
accessories.

Saks Fifth Avenue
The name says it all—perfect for
strolling and spending . . .
judiciously!

Salvation Army (main branch)
536 West 46th St.
This is thrift-shop central.

San Francisco Clothing
975 Lexington Ave.
Annie Hall forever—men and
women.

Second Act
1046 Madison Ave. (near 80th St.)
Children's resale shop with a good
selection, more for girls than
boys. Shoes, boots, records, and
books on sale, too.

Selva and Sons Inc.
1776 Broadway
Dance shoes, leotards, etc.

Sermoneta
740 Madison Ave.
South American market goods at
low prices. Wicker and clothes.

Simons
67 Third Ave. at 4th St.
Work clothes of all manufacturers.

Small Business
101 Wooster St.
Darling children's clothes.

Soho Canal Flea Market
369 Canal St. (near W. Broadway)
An indoor and outdoor market,
open year round, seven days a
week from 11 A.M. to 6 P.M.
Antiques, clothes, and collectables.

Sona
11 East 55th St.
East Indian clothing.

Spence Chapin Corner Shop
1065 Lexington Ave.
Unique beauties such as cashmere
overcoats, turn-of-the-century
embroidered Chinese coats.

Stitching Horse, Inc.
156 East 64th St.
Frye boots and handmade Stewart
cowboy boots from Arizona. Send
for free catalog.

Stone Free Kids
124 West 72nd St.
For children: original British
antique christening gowns,
functional American workwear,
full cowboy and girl outfits. The
owner, Sheila Gholson, travels the
world to find children's unusual
things.

Stuyvesant Square Thrift Shop
1430 Third Ave. (at 81st St.)
Big, airy sales floor, good supply of
furs and better women's clothes.

Sun Hi's Gift Co.
126 7th Ave. (between 17th and
18th Sts.)
Oriental gowns, lounge robes,
Hoppi coats, and bright padded
cotton jackets from China.

T. Anthony
772 Madison Ave.
Leather-trimmed canvas baggage
in classy colors.

Thrift House
39 West 57th St.
Offers delicious outfits at prices
well below many of the other thrift
shops.

Tibetan Arts & Crafts Ltd.
693 Madison Ave.
Tibetan shoes and wonderful
pointed-toe boots; fur and wool
hats with earflaps; fabrics,
sweaters, coats, and more.

T. O. Dey
509 Fifth Ave. (near 42nd St.)
8th Floor
Shoe and boot remodeling. Will
blunt or round off pointed toes,
change closed shoes to sandals,
change heel height and width.

Union Shirt Company, Inc.
915 Broadway
Makers of the West Point uniform
shirt.

Unique Clothing Warehouse
718 Broadway
One of the original Cheap Chic
hotspots, that now has branches in
department stores all over,
including Macy's.

Vandyke Hatters
848 Sixth Ave. (near 30th St.)
Westerns, berets—theatrical to
folksy. They can also block, clean,
and restore favorite hats.

Victoria Falls
170 Spring St.
White Victoriana: from wedding
gowns to sleep shifts in delectable
eyelets, embroideries, lace. Nice
blouses.

Weiss & Mahoney
142 Fifth Ave.
Almost every imaginable army-
surplus item down to women's
dress uniforms. The best all-
around assortment at the lowest
prices.

Wendy's Store
1046 Madison Ave.
Everything for the chic small one.

Woolworth's
34th St. (near 6th Ave.)
How about some cheap
accessories? Cartier-style tank
watch for a price anyone can
afford.

NEW YORK

OUTSIDE OF NEW YORK CITY

Gauze & Effect
19 Middle Neck Rd.
Great Neck

The Graduate Boutique
269 Main St.
Oneonta
Jeans, tops, jewelry, gifts, baskets,
lingerie, fur coats, jackets.

Hapiglop
Woodstock

Kimberley's
Main St.
Bridgehampton
Wonderful antiques, imports, and
scarf-kimonos.

Marsha's Mood Ltd.
470 Central Ave.
Cedarhurst

Old World Imports
21 Tinker St.
Woodstock

Three Eleven Shop
Walt Whitman Shopping Center
260-1 Route 110
Huntington

Zoom
10 Job's Lane
Southhampton
Some real Cheap Chic. Jan
Cushing's bikinis; Lee Radziwill's
T-shirts. Simple.

NORTH DAKOTA

Touch of Class
614 Kirkwood Plaza
Bismark

OHIO

Creative Fashions
2869 Chagrin Blvd.
Woodmere

Earth Rose
221 Xenia
Yellow Springs
Gifts and clothing from all over the
world. Hand-hammered Persian
copper jewelry from Greece. Indian
clothing (cheap).

OKLAHOMA

Cyrk & Company
50 Penn Pl.
Oklahoma City

Life Style Unlimited
3311 East 11th St.
Tulsa
Pure silk, cotton, and wool clothes
from China, Afghanistan, India,
Indonesia, and Africa, and jewelry.

Ms. Salon Hair Care Center
6221 East 61st St.
Tulsa
Linda James, makeup artist.

OREGON

Sinu's
9526 Washington Sq.
Portland

Sophisticate
917 S. Walden
Portland

PENNSYLVANIA

Bob Henicle & Company
534 Spruce St.
Scranton

Gimbels
Pittsburgh
Look for the Unique Clothing
Warehouse corner.

I. Goldberg's
8th & Chestnut Sts.
Philadelphia
University of Pennsylvania
students with army-navy surplus
for years.

Penn Center Army-Navy
20th & Market St.
Philadelphia
Standard army-navy supplies in the
heart of Philadelphia.

Scoop
227-233 Fifth Ave.
Pittsburgh

Stoney End Boutique
7608 City Line Ave.
Philadelphia

Straw Flowers
8138 Germantown Ave.
Philadelphia

TEXAS

Backstage Designs
802 W. Alabama St.
Houston
"For the woman who knows
fashion," personalized designs.

Beacon Company
4538 McKinney St.
Dallas
Check them for utilitarian clothing.

Big Tex Army-Navy Store
215 W. Jefferson St.
Dallas
Army-navy surplus items.

Contagious Clothing Co.
5362 Westheimer St.
Houston
Surplus and primo antique
clothing.

C.R. Adkins Army Store
5800 Maple St.
Dallas
And yet another army-navy store
to peruse for finds.

Las Manos, Inc.
12215 Coit Rd.
Dallas

Maharani
270 N. Anderson Lane
Austin

Neiman-Marcus
Main & Ervay Sts.
Dallas
To experience the best, as Stanley
Marcus envisioned it. Also in
Houston.

Stelzig's
Houston
Old, established store carrying
Tony Lama boots, Lucchese boots
made in San Antonio since 1883.
Basic Western clothes and
accessories.

Tootsie's
5350 Westheimer Rd. (near the
Galleria)
Houston
Basic European tops and bottoms;
unique accessories.

VERMONT

Phase One, Inc.
Waitsfield

Wings
38 Elliot St.
Brattleboro
An oasis of clothing consciousness:
silks from the Victorian times to
the fifties, jeans, accessories,
jewelry; natural fibers; custom-
made; small-time designers.

Yankee Notions
41 West Rd.
Bennington

VIRGINIA

Pennyante
Bragg St.
The Plains

Sautar Brothers, Inc.,
Department Store
629 Mercer St.
Princeton

WASHINGTON

Waitesmith's Photographic Styling
and Design
14 West Comstock
Seattle

WISCONSIN

Goldfish-U.S. Surplus
2103 W. North Ave.
Milwaukee
One of Milwaukee's favorite stores
for army-navy surplus.

PEX-U.S. Military Supply
533 West Wisconsin
Milwaukee
Another place to shop for army-
navy needs.

CANADA

Marni
55 Avenue Rd.
Toronto, Ontario

Northwest Handcraft House
110 West Esplanade
North Vancouver, B.C.

Robin
37 Hazelton Ave.
Toronto, Ontario

Tiangius
2505-1850 Lomax St.
Vancouver, B.C.

Valley Fibers Ltd.
51 William St.
Ottawa, Ontario
Folkwear.

England and France

ENGLAND
LONDON

Pick up a copy of Kaori O'Connor's
Fashion Guide (Coronet Books,
£1.25) at Janet Reger's on
Beauchamp Place or at a local
bookstore.

Antiquarius
135 King's Rd.
Flea market extraordinaire.

Badges & Equipment
Real English army-navy-RAF
surplus including flying suits,
paratrooper trousers, jungle hats,
and more.

Beauchamp Place
Check out the whole street:
Cannibal; Caroline Charles;
Deborah and Clare; Emeline;
Graffiti; Janet Reger; Janet Wilson;
Lucienne Philips; N. Peal; Piero de
Monzi.

Bill Gibb
138 New Bond St.

Bochamba
104 Fulham Rd.

The Body Shop
King's Road punk.

Brother Sun
171 Fulham Rd.

Brown's
27 South Molton St.

Burberry's
18 Haymarket

Bus Stop
3 Kensington Church St.
Cheap chic.

C & A (Marble Arch)
505 Oxford St.
Fastest with the latest at the
lowest.

Captain OM Watts
45 Albemarle St.
For yachtsmen.

Carolyn Brunn
4 South Molton St.

Chelsea Cobbler
54 King's Rd.
Not to be confused with the store
in New York. This is the original.

Elle
92 New Bond St.
. . .if you're not going to proceed to
Paris.

Fiorucci
15 Brompton Rd.

Fortnum and Mason
181 Piccadilly Circus

Gibb's
38 Floral St.
All sorts of fascinating shops.

Harrod's
Knightsbridge
You can buy the English edition of
Cheap Chic here, along with just
about everything.

H. Huntsman and Son
11 Savile Row
Made-to-measure clothes,
including riding, hunting, and
jockey clothes.

Jaeger
204 Regent St.
Sweaters.

Janet Reger
Beauchamp Place
Lingerie.

Jap and Joseph
20 Brompton Rd.
Kenzo et al.

Joseph
13 South Molton St.

Kickers
66 South Molton St.

King's Road: Look for Ace; Joanna's
Tent; Ladies Habits; Meeny's.

Kurt Geiger
95 New Bond St.
Italian shoes and boots. Expensive.

Laurence Corner
62 Hampstead Rd.
Genuine army-navy surplus.

Liberty
210 Regent St.
The classic Liberty prints.

Lobb
Tops for men's shoes.

Marks & Spencer
458 Oxford St.
Large department store, great for
sweaters and children's clothes.

Mary Farrin
9 South Molton St.

Mrs. Howie
138 Longacre
Covent Garden area.
New shops constantly pop up.

N. Peal
54 Burlington Arcade

Piero di Monzi
70 Fulham Rd.

Portobello Road Market
Street market open Friday and
Saturday (Saturday is the best).
Antiques, clothing, and lots more
to see.

Scotch House
2 Brompton Rd.
Knightsbridge

Seditionaries
King's Road punk.

Stirling Cooper
94 New Bond St.

Thea Porter
8 Greek St.

Le Trousseau
64 Blandford St.
Sexy lingerie (all the way to
38DD!), plus handmade sewn-to-
measure delicacies.

Turnbull and Asser
21 Jermyn St. or
23 Bury St.
Fine, classic British men's clothing,
custom-made and ready-to-wear.

Zapata Shoes
49 Old Church St.
(off King's Road)
Shoes designed by Manolo
Blahnik...always one step ahead
of the game.

FRANCE

PARIS

Department stores

Galeries Lafayette
40 Blvd. Haussmann

Marche Aux Puces
(street markets in Paris)
Marche St. Pierre—good selection
of fabrics, old and new
Montmartre
Porte St. Ouen
Mairie de Montreuil—good
bargains; arrive by 7 A.M.

Printemps
64 Blvd. Haussmann

Prisunic
109 rue de la Boetie

Samaritaine
18 rue de la Monnaie

Boutiques: Right Bank

A la Blouse des Halles
140, rue de Faubourg St. Martin
Coveralls, jewelers' smocks, and
butchers' jackets—plus more.

Azzaro
65 Faubourg St. Honoré
For fancy, fancy evenings.

Caracalla
95 rue de Longchamp
Silky underthings.

Charles Jourdan
5 Blvd. de la Madeleine
10 Faubourg St. Honoré

Dianne B.
Les Halles
Also a boutique on Madison
Avenue in New York.

France Andrevie
2 Place des Victoires

Indian Trading Post
Passage Choiseul
For American Indian-Western gear
in Paris.

Issey Miyake
38 Place du Marche St. Honoré
Domaine of the supercreator.

J.C. Castelbajac
31 Place du Marche St. Honoré

Jean Dinh Van
7 rue de la Paix
Gold jewelry.

Jungle Jap
3 Place des Victoires
Kenzo's domaine.

Madame Cadolle
14 rue Cambon
Fine example of French lingerie.

La Maison Bleue
1 rue du Marché St. Honoré

Les Nuits d'Elodie
Avenue MacMahon
Sexy lingerie.

Pablo and Delia
30 Place du Marché St. Honoré

Poiray
8 rue de la Paix
More gold jewelry.

Pulcinella
10 rue Vignon
Old jewelry.

Repetto
Place de L'Opera
French equivalent of Capezio.
Ballet supplies, leotards, etc.
Excellent "off-color" selection.

Roger Vivier
24 rue François 1er
Where Diana Vreeland's shoes
come from.

Soldes magazine
3, Place Malesherbes
Send for this—every month it lists
the best bargains in each of Paris's
twenty districts, with emphasis on
unique, quality items.

Sotovol
125, rue du Faubourg St. Martin
Ideal for jumpsuits. They cater to
racing car drivers, aviators, etc.

Thierry Muggler
10 Place des Victoires

Yves St. Laurent
38 Faubourg St. Honoré
(shoes at 58)

Boutiques: Left Bank

Andrea Pfister
56 rue du Four

L'Autre Jour
26 Avenue de la Bourdonnais
Antique clothing.

C.A.A.
45 rue de Rennes
Chinese imports, period clothes.

Carola
27 rue du Four

Centre Maine Montparnasse
3 rue de l'Arrivée

Chacok
18 rue de Grenelle

Exactement Fauve
5 rue Princesse

Fabrice
26 rue Bonaparte

François Villon
58 rue Bonaparte

Globe (The Khaki Rush)
12, rue Pierre Lescot
Army clothes, Chinese and
Japanese workers' pants and
kimonos; newest looks from old
favorites.

Jardins d'Orient
11 rue du Dragon

Jeanne d'O
Antique jewelry.

Maude Frizon
83 rue des St. Peres
Shoes (also in NYC).

Mezzo Mezzo
21 rue du Dragon

Mic Mac
13 rue de Tournon

Missoni
79 rue du Rennes

Moons
48 rue de Verneuil

Nuage
7 rue du Cherche Middi
Old clothes.

Sabbia Rosa
71 rue des St. Peres
Lingerie.

Sasha
24 rue de Buci
Shoes.

Sonia Rykiel
6 rue de Grenelle

Tango
26 rue de Rennes

Ter et Bantine
5 rue de Vieux Colombier

Thea Porter
15 rue de Tournon

UFO
8 rue de Grenelle

La Vie en Rose
27 rue de l'Abbe Gregoire

Western House
23 rue des Canettes

Shopping by Mail

Acadian Crafts Association
P.O. 29
St. Catherine St.
Madawaski, Maine 04756
Hand-crocheted French-Acadian
crafts—ladies' wear and infants's
clothing. Well priced.

Adam York
340 Poplar St.
Hanover, Pennsylvania 17331
Gifts, clothes, jewelry. Everything
from colorful hard hats to stuffed
dolls with the face of your choice.

American Express Gift Catalog
P.O. Box 754
Great Neck, New York 11025
Unusual items: Japanese screens,
small heart-shaped diamond
necklaces, canvas bags.

A. S. Cooper & Cons, Ltd.
37 Front St.
Hamilton, Bermuda
Classic shetland crew-neck
sweaters in fifteen colors. Other
classics.

Austin-Hall Company
P.O. Box 12368
El Paso, Texas 79912
Custom western boots. Good
quality, cheap price.

Belgian Shoes
60 East 56th St.
New York, New York 10022
Soft hand-turned moccasins for
men and women.

Bergdorf Goodman
754 Fifth Ave.
New York, New York 10019
Exclusive items, fine designer
clothing, and accessories.

Bloomingdale's Home/Living
Catalog
1000 Third Ave.
New York, New York 10022

Bombay Britches
Box 637
Bronxville, New York
(914) 961-4553
Money back guarantee on Bombay
britches, French army surplus,
authentic journeyman mason's
book bag, imprinted sushi tins from
Japan. "Good goods at a good price"
is their credo. All postage, tax, and
handling included.

Bonwit Teller
721 Fifth Ave.
New York, New York 10022

Brentano's
586 Fifth Ave.
New York, New York 10036
Books, games, gifts, jewelry.

Brooks Brothers
346 Madison Ave.
New York, New York 10017
Ivy Leaguer's delight.

Brownstone Studio
342 Madison Ave.
New York, New York 10017
Classic fashion items and
accessories.

Budget Uniform Center, Inc.
1613 Chestnut St.
Philadelphia, Pennsylvania 19103
Sixty-page color catalog mailed
three times a year. Uniforms in
white and colors; jackets, lab coats.

Camalier & Buckley
1141 Connecticut Ave.
Washington, D.C. 20036
Gift items: leather shopping bag,
hippopotamus planter, pig-shaped
cookie jar.

Capezio Dance Catalog
1841 Broadway
New York, New York 10023
Full line of dance clothes and
accessories. Ask for the store
nearest you.

Castello
836 Broadway
New York, New York 10003
Send for fencing equipment
catalog, or combative sports
catalog...judo coats, Kung Fu
suits, etc.

Caswell-Massey Co., Ltd.
320 West 13th St.
New York, New York 10014
Hand-illustrated, old-fashioned
toiletry catalog. Rare imported
soaps, hair & scalp care, potpourri,
and aromatics, etc.

Chris-Craft
Algonae, Michigan 48001
"Good life" equipment: from sailing
attire to jewelry, suede tennis
shoes to binoculars.

The Chocolate Soup
249 East 77th St.
New York, New York 10021
The Danish Souperbag in gray,
chocolate brown, or bright blue
waterproof canvas.

Danskin, Inc.
1114 Avenue of the Americas
New York, New York 10036
Tops, bodysuits, hosiery, and
dancewear for men, women, and
children. Ask for the store in your
area.

Dunham's of Maine
20 Castongway Sq.
Waterville, Maine 04901
Classic designs for men and women
in pure cottons, silks, linen, and
wool.

Echo Scarf Company
485 Fifth Ave.
New York, New York 10017
(212) 682-5430
Write or phone for store near you
that carries their 27-in. square,
white, thin handkerchief; cottons.

Empire
443 Broadway
New York, New York 10013
Fifties leather jackets, chenille
emblems, all sorts of uniforms.

Everlast Sport
750 East 132nd St.
Bronx, New York 10454
Boxing equipment, including
shorts and robes.

Folkwear Ethnic Patterns
Box 98
Forestville, California 95936
Catalogs.

Frederick's of Hollywood
6608 Hollywood Blvd.
Hollywood, California
Longtime mail-order leader in
"sexy chic"...worth reading, even
if you don't order. Had perhaps the
first "string" bathing suits; lots
more.

Fulton Supply Co., Inc.
23 Fulton St.
New York, New York 10038

Gatsby's
P.O. Box 11723
Atlanta, Georgia 30305

Greek Island, Ltd.
215 East 49th St.
New York, New York 10017
Cotton voile or gauze scarves;
cotton tops, skirts, and caftans.

Hammacher Shlemmer
147 East 57th St.
New York, New York 10022
Gifts: espresso makers (chrome or
gold-plated); cordless, portable
telephones that run on batteries.
Not cheap.

Haucraft from Europe
P.O. Box 372
Sausalito California 94965
Folk wear.

Holubar
Dept. 4-119H Box 7
Boulder, Colorado 80302
Down jackets and parkas; also,
duffel bags.

Honeybee
2745 Philmont Ave.
Huntingdon Valley,
Pennsylvania 19006
Classic, fancy, casual, and
loungewear.

Horchow Collection
P.O. 34257
Dallas, Texas 75234
A collection of exclusive big-city
status possessions. A must for the
sensuous shopper.

Hunting World
16 East 53rd St.
New York, New York 10022
Safari central; great canvas.

I. Buss Uniform & Co., Inc.
50 West 17th St.
New York, New York 10011
Mid-calf slicker with
corduroy collar.

I. Goldberg & Company Army-
Navy
902 Chestnut St.
Philadelphia, Pennsylvania 19107
Scarlet wool French beret $4.25.

I. Magnin
P.O. Box 7660
San Francisco, California 94120
High style—designer clothes by
mail!

J. Capps & Sons, Ltd.
1180 Sunrise Valley Dr.
Reston, Virginia 22091
Body- armor disguised as vests,
sport coats, T-shirts, etc. Just the
thing for revolutions.

J.C. Penny Co., Inc.
1301 Avenue of the Americas
New York, New York 10019
Big fall and spring catalogs. Very
stylish too.

Janet Reger
2 Beauchamp Pl. SW3
33 Brook St. W.2
London, England
Catalog $4. Beautiful pure silk
designer lingerie, night wear.

Joe Hall Boots
P.O. Box 17971
El Paso, Texas
Fine Western boots made to order,
with custom details.

Kaleidoscope
2201 Faulkner Road, N.E.
Atlanta, Georgia 30324
Gifts! Unusual ivory jewelry; clock
with personalized message on its
face; leisure clothes and kitchen
accessories.

Kaufman & Sons
139 E. 24th St.
New York, New York 10010
To keep your feet dry—elastic-
sided jodphur boots. All riding
clothes.

Kreeger & Son
16 W. 46th Street
New York, New York 10017
Outdoor clothing. Good deal on
wool rag sweaters; heavy cotton
"chamois" shirts. Good-quality
down jackets.

L. L. Bean, Inc.
Freeport, Maine 04032
100 percent wool-plaid shirts, wool
jackets, everything you'll ever need
for the outdoor, sportive life.